COMING HOME TO DIVINE PRESENCE

SACRED PRINCIPLES TO EMBODY YOUR GREATEST LIGHT

Tiara Kumara

IAMAvatar.org

info@iamavatar.org

ISBN 13: 978-1-7955-2695-1
ISBN 10: 1-7955-2695-1

Dedicated to the awakened emergence of
Divine Love, Wisdom, and the Power of Will
inside each human heart.

CONTENTS

PREFACE

The solution to human suffering can never be found within a focus that is placed upon the limited nature of the personal self or the false world of appearances.

The great Buddha spoke of this world as being like a bubble on the ocean, an illusion that would pass away just as surely as it had appeared. He taught that the spiritual aspirant should not become attached to it in any way.

Jesus the Christ said, "My Kingdom is not of this world" and he urged everyone to seek ye first that Kingdom and then all shall be given.

There is nothing in the material realm of the ego that has the redeeming power to lift the imprisoned soul from all its ignorance.

The solution to the pain of the human heart and its sufferings can be perceived through a focus on what is already perfect, whole and complete. This is a solution that places the attention upon the greater, and that which liberates.

It is through a sincere and humble seeking of that, which has always been true and forever will be true. This truth is not of this reality of time and space, where everything is in a perpetual state of change.

Absolute truth cannot be written or even spoken about. It can only be experienced.

The way to experience absolute truth, and to be liberated by it, is to completely and unconditionally give up all ideas and beliefs about the personal self.

Not our will but 'Thy Will' be done.

All who wish to return to the divine reality must first become empty of self, ever so humble and ready to be filled with the living light of truth, even though sometimes it may be hard to bear.

We must die to the old self and move into unchartered territory. This is through the wilderness of an inner journey to eventually find our way home.

The path leading to the front door can be a long and arduous one, fraught with many thorns. There is however, a gentler way.

This is to align with your imperishable identity and the immortal nucleus of your entire existence.

With this as your daily mirror, there will be no limits to what you can do and accomplish.

"There is no greater power than the Divine Presence within me."

INTRODUCTION

THE GREATER YOU

The entire universe is propelled through the energy of a living field of intelligence of which everything and everyone is an integral part.

All life in our system of worlds exists within this infinitely expanding intelligence, which we might refer to as Prime Creator, God, or Absolute Source.

This consciousness field of source intelligence also incarnates into physical reality. It embodies as a living, breathing and thinking entity, individualized within each human soul's formed expression.

This supremely intelligent presence is the source point for every single person. It is the central essence of one's being, the God within.

It explains why we, as humans who are made in the image and likeness of this all-pervasive transcendent field, can create from within our own microcosm and simply through the mechanism of thought.

When words are used like the greater self, higher mind, atman, and our multidimensional nature, all of these big identities converge and meld into an inclusive whole. This wholeness is a unique expression of pure awareness, or "presence" that is outwardly reflecting into the world of matter.

This presence is absolutely divine, no matter what form it takes. It is an all-pervading, intelligent and loving force of benevolent energy within and throughout all manifested creation. This Divine Presence is our source of life.

We each have an individualized Divine Presence, which guides our life both as a sovereign being and a unified whole. It is within us and is who we really are as a totality of consciousness.

We are divinity in the form, each and every single person on this planet. We are all part of this great Divine Presence as one being, rhythmically pulsing.

This book presents ideas about how to practically integrate and express your self, simply and purely, as an individualized Divine Presence.

The idea of a personal Divine Presence can be defined as the non-physical component of your human embodiment that serves as a conduit to all other versions and dimensions of your one total and very vast self.

The all-inclusive Divine Presence, housed within you, is the intermediary that distills information from the spiritual realms in a way that your personality can understand. It functions like a translator, relaying higher dimensional information to be readily deciphered and applied.

This is your voice of conscience that reveals through your personality when you are in attunement with its inspiring influence. What you receive and how you receive is directly linked to your phase of evolutionary development.

In truth, you are a unique spark of light that permanently resides within the vast body called God awareness, the intelligence of all existence. You are an aspect of this creation field experiencing itself in a physical form. Wholeness resides within you. You have never ever been separated.

This pathway you are now upon is fundamentally called, "the great awakening". This ultimately leads into a grounded and practical emergence of the embodied state of divine immanence.

To be operating from a state of divine immanence is to know, without any fiber of doubt, that the omnipresent nature of God permeates all aspects of your life. You can learn how to maneuver within these potent currents and give high levels of outer service.

What is God? Well, that idea is yours to define. One thing is for certain. You are made in its image and likeness.

In this phase of your evolutionary leap, your microcosmic human is going macro. This is continual expansion into bigger and bigger expressions of you, as a great radiant being.

This is what self-actualization is all about. You are making a grand return to the realization of your truer, greater self.

You have never lost this realization; it has simply been covered up in the layers of maya from the density of physical incarnation. Maya is another word for illusion. This illusion is the game and what God, expressing through your unique channel, obviously wants to experience.

It is, however, the interpenetration of this divine essence and activity within you that inspires you with the burning passion to experience the mystery that lies beyond the veil of human illusion.

YOU ARE DIVINE PRESENCE

"Divine Presence" is your true nature. You are an imperishable, eternal and individualized identity that is also a part of every other human being.

As the highest aspect of your vast multidimensional constitution, the Divine Presence is the original seed of love and the immortal nucleus of your entire existence.

It is the originating source of every constructive impulse, thought, feeling, breath and action. Its unifying, cohesive nature is the source of all of the love, wisdom and power required to overcome absolutely anything and everything that is of discordance and limitation.

The most beautiful realization of all is that your Divine Presence, as the greater you, is constantly extending its hand and providing you with an exact template to match. It is all around you. It is always reflecting the mirror image of your ultimate potential.

This influencing reflection is what motivates your strongest passions and your deepest desires. It is what has brought you to be right here and right now.

You and this transcendent expression are one fused consciousness. There is no separation. You have always been self-realized. You already *are* divinely human.

Everything comes from your consciousness. Everything is part of the one body of omnipresent awareness. Walk in this truth and there will be no limits to what you can do and achieve.

When you know the self and the Divine Presence to be one, unified entity, all of your aligned intentions is quickly accomplished. It is from this state of knowing, that every question is answered and every thought that you think produces a vibration that coheres your energy.

To know yourself at the deepest level is to simultaneously know and experience the Divine Presence manifesting in your life. As a result, this becomes the pure mirror of your thought energy.

As you develop intimate relationship with and give constant attention to your Divine Presence, seeming miracles begin to happen. This includes such occurrences as instant manifestation, pristine clarity and spontaneous transformation.

This transpires simply through the constancy of your unwavering focus placed upon the greater you. In doing so, spiritual energy around you intensifies and expands as the points of light within every cell of your flesh body respond in tremendous gratitude.

God, expressing as the Divine Presence within you, is the authority of the entire universe. The Divine Presence hears, sees, thinks, feels and responds only to perfection on its level of cosmic service.

As you consistently give adoration, feel gratitude and qualify your every activity through this energy stream, your daily positive daily impact upon life is immeasurable.

With all of us self-actualizing as Divine Presence, we coherently serve as a universal Divine Presence, operating within all cosmic dimensions and radiating the patterns of the perfection of God in action.

With more and more people coming home to Divine Presence, imagine the tremendous impact this is having upon our shifting world.

"When I stand unified with Divine Principle, all is magnetized to me in spontaneous flow, in perfect timing and in just the right quantity. No strenuous effort is required."

THE EMERGING RACE:
A PRODIGY OF PRINCIPLE

There are many laws of nature that govern the natural phenomena of our physical reality. We are exploring some of these driving principles and their unerring nature to help clarify our advancing steps on the spiritual path.

Consciously harmonizing with their tremendous, unwavering power, with clear and focused intention, can mean the difference between a life filled with struggle and pain or one of sustained joy and a profound sense of peace and fulfillment.

The emerging consciousness that we are birthing, as an enlightened collective, has been called by many names. Numerous labels are used such as the new root race, Divine-Humans, Avatar Blueprint, Christ Consciousness, Unity Consciousness, and so forth.

These terms all refer to an evolved human nature that has transitioned from duality-based programming into unified awareness. This can be described as an expanded human awareness that lives and thrives from its coherence with an awakened collective consciousness.

This follows the natural course of conscious evolution, from the divisive human personality into a cohesive, interconnected whole.

The one single characteristic of this new consciousness that drastically differs from the current human mindset is that it lives in accordance with divine principle. These are the laws of nature that are the foundation stones upon which humanity's new framework of consciousness is built.

In fact, these are the same principles that govern every aspect of the universe and are the means by which our world, solar system, galaxy and the entire cosmos continues to exist, thrive and expand.

In essence, the universal laws of nature are great spiritual truths. They are the governing influences that determine every aspect of creation. This includes each of the events, conditions and circumstances experienced by you, me and everyone else in the world, on both an individual and mass scale.

It is in the divine, or metaphysical principle, along with the understanding of how energy truly flows that awakens our greater abilities to co-create from higher dimensional templates. This can only be done while using a new system of thought.

Knowing and using some of the more relevant universal principles can enable and empower great depths of personal transformation. These timeless principles are the stepping-stones into full alchemical union with your Divine Presence.

We all have the inner power to change any condition in our lives that is not in resonance with our preferred reality. Higher vibration always consumes and transforms lower vibration.

Therefore, we can shift any undesired energies by understanding the universal principle and applying the principles in such a way to effect positive change.

For example, there are many great spiritual truths that apply to our phases of new thought unification, especially as this concerns the authentic, embodied realization of Divine Presence.

Throughout this book, many of these spiritual principles are given high importance. There is one universal truth, however, that is the 'foundation stone' to divine embodiment. This is the Law of Correspondence.

THE LAW OF CORRESPONDENCE

There is conscious life everywhere, all made from the exact same core substance. All things in the universe are infinitely interconnected. No matter what form of energy is presenting itself, everything is representing the larger whole.

There is a popular saying, "As above so below, as within so without". This adage speaks to the principle of correspondence and the mirror-image relationship between all that exists in the cosmos. It simply says that the greater and the lesser are alike. It conveys that, in all existence, the common interweaving threads between the dimensions of manifestation are harmony, agreement and correspondence.

Everything is a microcosm of the macrocosm. We see the same patterns reproduced in all levels of the cosmos, from the largest scale all the way down to the smallest sub-atomic substance, including the metaphysical.

The universe and the Earth are of the same pattern. Nature and man are of the same pattern. Our outer world is nothing more than a reflection of our inner world. By observing one relation, we gain knowledge of the reflected whole.

The universe is part of 'All That Is', which is the same as God, the ultimate creator intelligence. All conscious life is made from the exact same core substance. This substance is vibrating through patterns of energy, light and sound.

This core vibrational pattern of the ultimate principal entity is the same as the human. The human pattern is the same as the cell. The cell's vibrational pattern is the same as the atom.

This idea expresses that humans are made in the image and likeness of the one original Creator of everything, at the most macro level. All forms of life are birthed from this one primary source. All is a reflection and a stepped down version of its greater aspect.

Consciousness is at the core of even the simplest of life. For example, we can consider the innate cognition in the very nucleus of the globular atom.

For years, scientists have known that atoms are intelligently driven particles of energy that can discriminate and choose. Atoms possess cognitive qualities such as the ability to select and reject, to attract and repulse. They also demonstrate the abilities of sensation, movement and desire.

The concept of the atom as an intelligent energy is very much like human psychology, only that the atom's existence is within a more limited radius and circumscribed degree. We can view ourselves as the greater human atom representing the total intelligence of all of our bodily atoms.

Just as our physical bodies are made up of spinning atoms, all of our individual human forms cohere together to form an even greater atomic body. This evolved entity comprises the sum total of an intelligently driven group consciousness.

The evolved group atom and its unifying nature demonstrate further as planetary consciousness, which is the sum total of all of the groups and states of awareness. The evolution of the intelligent planetary atom continues on into solar consciousness forming an even greater entity. It expands next into galactic consciousness, then into universal space and beyond.

At each successive stage, the atom evolves into greater and more encompassing fields of intelligence that eventually returns to the consciousness of the Creator Deity Itself. From macro to micro, everything is a representation of the larger whole and part of a deeper reality where all things in the universe are infinitely interconnected.

The cosmic principle of correspondence shows that all planes of existence function after the same rules and patterns. There is a very close relationship between the human being as a microcosm and its God parent as the macrocosm.

To put it more directly, you are an aspect of God in the flesh. Your consciousness is born from and permanently resides within the vast macrocosmic body called God awareness, or existence itself; the primary source from which everything emanates.

This great Divine Presence that lives inside of you, is the same force of energy that creates everything from atoms and stars to the DNA of all life. You are a microcosm made in the image of the macrocosm, and essentially, an aspect of God outpictured in physical form.

You are within God and God is within you. You are one unified whole. The sum total of all of your thoughts, actions and beliefs is the way that God expresses itself through the unique gateway that is you, as a human channel.

Each and every form of life in physical reality reflects all of the different ways that the infinite Creator has of expressing itself, every single bit of it! Do you see, now, that you are perfect and whole and always have been?

Now, consider that every single particle of your being exists in pure love. It is the strongest cohesive bond that you have with your Creator and absolutely nothing can break this apart.

What we are doing in this great spiritual awakening is remembering who we really are and how to transition into our greater potential as Divine Presence. We are learning how to rise up and out of limitation by shifting into a new structure of thought. We are leaving the program of suffering and returning home to our true nature, all the while maintaining our physicality.

When we do this for ourselves, we actually assist the entire human race to do this as well. Our accomplishment of self-realization is very contagious and serves as a powerfully radiating force of love. This love permeates and transforms all existence.

One of the best ways to rise out of limitation is to always remember that you are the creator in the physical reality. Your current reality is a mirror to what is going on inside of you. Your current reality has manifested as a result of your innermost dominant thoughts.

Practice shifting your mind's default by consistently placing your focus upon the greater, and with the highest version of who you really are. Then, allow that greater self, your beloved Divine Presence, to be the one and only navigator of your life.

Reality reflects your state of mind.

State of mind reflects your reality.

"By affirming my intentions through positive daily action, a magnetic field of resonance completely shifts towards that intention. I am highly productive as an active co-creator in the manifestation process."

THE ACTION
OF INTENT

The previous chapter likened the emerging race consciousness to a 'prodigy of principle', which coheres to the fundamental universal laws of energy. These principles serve
as the foundational stepping-stones to human evolution.

Another principle that is of great significance to our evolutionary
advancement is referred to as the Law of Action. This principle
must be applied in order for us to manifest in the physical reality.

It is not only about thinking the thoughts or having the dream.
It is also necessary to take the specific action steps that support
our intentions and highest held visions.

English physicist and mathematician, Sir Isaac Newton, first presented his laws of motion in 1686. One of these laws states, that
for every action (force) in nature there is an equal and opposite
reaction. He used the example that if object A exerts a force on
object B, then likewise, object B also exerts an equal and opposite force on object A.

This same principle holds true for our personal intentions. When
appropriate action is exerted upon our intentions, an inevitable
reaction is experienced.

To take action means to take the actual physical steps towards the desired outcome. Action, along with positive intention, is what brings our dreams and innermost visions to life. Only by taking actions that correspond with the clarity of intention will the universe know what to bring into your life.

When you take affirmative action steps, from the simplest to the grandest, you are sending a tremendous message to the universal creation field. You set into motion the corresponding effects that mold your immediate future.

By affirming your intentions through positive daily action, a magnetic field of resonance completely shifts towards that intention and impressive results will most likely be experienced. This universal principle teaches us to be productive and active co-creators in the manifestation process.

Of all of the universal principles, the Law of Action is one of the most underused and overlooked. Without action, there is no reaction, thus, no foreseeable results. It is in the consistent application of the Law of Action that many people falter when pursuing achievement.

Obstacles such as fears and doubts, laziness and procrastination are common ones that block the way. Whatever the case, it is the lack of motion that casts a shadow upon all of the dormant and unrealized dreams and visions.

APPLYING THE PRINCIPLE

The very first action in the manifestation process is the setting of intention. To have an intention is to have purpose. To have intent is to know the meaning behind what you do.

This book lays out how to authentically embody your greater self-expression. Devote quality time to contemplate your intentions and to find clarity of purpose for this sacred endeavor.

This is an opportune moment to really be honest with yourself, while looking deeply into your motivations. You want to make sure that all of this is very real for your life, so real that you are willing to dedicate your full focus and commitment. This is what it will take to genuinely embody your highest potential.

The prime Vedic doctrine of self-realization, known as the Upanishads states,

"You are what your deepest desire is. As your desire is, so is your intention. As your intention is, so is your will. As your will is, so is your deed. As your deed is, so is your destiny."

Most likely you were drawn here because of the attraction to what this book reflects, to embody and reveal your Divine Presence.

So often, spiritual aspirants yearn for deeper connection with the greater self and to know the life purpose and soul plan. There is a longing to feel and acknowledge the greater expression in a much more tangible and noticeable way so one can truly thrive from this resonance.

You might also be motivated by a desire to give higher levels of outer service, both to those around you and also to humanity. Yet, you are unclear as to how to go about doing this. (This is a big one.) At the end of the day, most of us just want to be giving service to others and to support humanity's consciousness shift.

Yes to all of these. These yearnings and desires are what spiritual aspirants project every day and are what have truly inspired the writing of this book.

The entire focus throughout this presentation is to help you:

» Deepen in connection with your higher power

» Authentically embody this supreme Presence

» Give higher quality service to others

This all sounds truly wonderful, yet, what comes in the way of this? How exactly do we forge a new pathway to truly realize our greater potential, rather than just dreaming about it or living through the mental concepts of others?

To begin formulating your specific intentions for this experience, give the devoted time to deeply contemplate the meaning behind what you are doing as an initiate on the spiritual path.

You are invited to look specifically at what might be hindering or blocking your advancement. Ponder upon any resistance, fears, doubts or any other programming that you carry. Look at any and all possibilities that prevent allowance of your greater expression to be securely anchored in the driver's seat.

Following are some common areas of challenge.

Ask yourself...

> » Do I often slide back into divisive and separating responses?
> » Is it challenging to express self-confidence and empowerment?
> » Do I often settle for mediocrity, or do not finish a previously inspired plan?
> » What am I really seeking?

Clarity of your intentions and then grounding them firmly in your conscious awareness will set the infinite organizing flow of your Divine Presence into its every fulfilling action.

The best part about setting intention is that your real work is done. This is because you are not the one ultimately in charge of how the intention manifests. This is the job of your Divine Presence.

Leave behind any worries about the details. An aggressive, "work real hard" attitude is not necessary. Simply hand these intentions over to your higher power.

Rest any concern and know firmly that your intention now lives as a seed in the fertile ground of pure potentiality. The maturation of these seeds of intention will reveal in absolute divine timing, always in accordance to your highest good and evolutionary plan.

As ego-driven personalities, we often overlook the real possibility that something else could be in charge. We are so accustomed to forcing our way through things. Some of us carry unconscious patterning that sets up an inner dialogue that life is hard and always involves a degree of suffering.

In our consciousness shift, we are learning the art of 'being' rather than nose-to-the-grind doing, doing, and doing. When we learn how to intimately align and harmonize our chosen way of being with Divine Presence, we discover just how simple and fun creating results can be.

Your only real job is to clearly define the why and the what. The role of the your great Divine Presence is to reveal the when and the how.

"Initiation is my greatest life quest. As I learn and expand, I experience greater levels of truth and greater levels of the one true self to experience."

INITIATION OF THE
HUMAN SOUL

This chapter gives a thorough review on the principle of initiation from the level of a soul perspective.

These ideas might seem fundamental, however, it is very beneficial to periodically revisit the basic principles of what we are doing in this grand intention of divine embodiment.

The purpose of this sharing is to help you remain clear and pristinely aligned with your highest purpose for incarnation. Hopefully, this review will give great support to your spiritual awakening and intentions for deeper development.

The idea of 'initiation' generally means to take new action or to put something into momentum. From a spiritual perspective, initiation can be likened to a rite of passage, which transitions us into a more expanded phase of personal development.

Most of us are familiar with what initiation means from first hand experience and from all of the seeming marathons we have endured in our spiritual process work.

The principle of soul initiation is set into motion from the important understanding that progressive and monitored initiation is absolutely necessary in order to advance into expanded consciousness.

Let's explore this understanding in great depth.

INITIATION OF THE HUMAN SOUL

It is said that planet Earth is the greatest schoolroom for the soul in this entire system of worlds. The story goes on to say that there are countless numbers of celestial souls lined up waiting to incarnate onto this extraordinary world stage.

Quite simply, the purpose of the earthly embodiment is for the soul to gain the needed experiences to evolve. Every person on Earth is here for this reason, to learn and to expand. Many entities choose to incarnate on Earth because of the speed and the intensity that important lessons and abilities can be realized.

We may ask; where does initiation come from?

It was through divine dispensation that the "Path of Spiritual Initiation" was created to become the planetary right of all sentient beings. It was designed by the guardians of the race to guarantee the surest and most accelerated method for human evolution from the Earth plane and its dense facade of separation.

This plan has been in effect since the darkest hours of Earth's history when the human race lost all contact with their core divine essence. It has been through great levels of divine intervention and the cohesive power of sustaining love that has made human evolution possible to this very day.

This divine intervention from many cosmic influences gifts the "Path of Spiritual Initiation" to any person who is expressing the desire to understand their life more fully. As soon as this type of inner questioning occurs, the human spirit naturally begins its journey of initiation to quicken its evolution.

You can think back to your own initial awakening and the process of self-inquiry, which helped to switch on the inner light. For many of us, it was the deep inner inquiry that asked questions like, who am I, where am I, what am I and what does all of this really mean?

If there were no pathway for initiation, the processes involved in the purification and preparation of the human soul for evolutionary advancement would be unimaginably slow. There would also be great instability along the way.

Initiation is like turning on the cosmic lighthouse. It provides a precise blueprint and finely tuned orchestrated plan for the gradual expansion of consciousness to occur.

This highly customized plan for each person's advancement occurs through successive stages of consciousness awakening, which support remembrance and re-unification. This puts a person face to face with the many temptations of life. This can be like a series of tests to determine how the gift of personal free will is adeptly handled.

To make continual upgrades while on the path, constant renunciation of all that is false, unreal and out of integrity with personal truth is required.

The fact is, that as we evolve, our inner truth changes. This is why initiation is a dynamic lifelong experience of self-realization. As we learn and expand, we experience greater levels of truth and greater levels of the one true self to experience.

Everyone's path is uniquely different and is part of the individual soul's divine design and evolutionary plan. Through initiation, we are lead step by step through an immense consciousness shift to eventually liberate the self from unresolved karma. Initiation also releases us from the shadow aspects and divisive tendencies of the human program.

During this journey, we literally undergo a transfiguration of our entire body vehicle and its energy system. Holiness of character is often the outcome of a great expansion of consciousness, which we, ourselves, attain through our commitment, dedication and steadfast endeavor on the long and often arduous path of initiation.

It is a new level of consciousness that is achieved and experienced as a result of coherent thought, aligned action and resulting service to others.

It is when we demonstrate our unwavering stewardship of the light and when our personal will is fused with Divine Will that we are given more responsibility. This is key to our advancement.

Through the greater Will, we are specifically groomed into light bearers of world service. The more that our consciousness expands, the greater responsibility we are given to serve larger and larger fields of energy.

This is the principle of initiation in these now times. We simply cannot experience self-realization without also being in service to assist the whole of the human race.

INITIATION IS LIFE

Once we wake up from the deep slumber of forgetfulness; initiation becomes our life... and greatest life quest. There is no escaping it.

Once you are on the path, there is no turning back, no matter how much you desire to once again lead a normal life. You quickly discover that there is no such thing as "normal". The normal you once knew is now seen as an illusion!

Much has indeed changed since the days when seekers and progressing aspirants took their initiations during a time when spiritual subject matter was considered taboo. It was rare to find any books, teachers or anything supportive of the inner quest.

It is why many secret societies and mystery schools were created to help advance these sacred studies from within hidden places. Spiritual initiates used to get burned at the stake for merely talking about anything metaphysical.

There was a great need to protect the ancient knowledge from the sinister forces on the planet that attempted to eliminate these teachings from the Earth. They knew the mass awakening of humanity would mean losing their dominion over the race.

Because of the massive shifts in energy now occurring on our planet, the mystery schools are no longer needed. All has come into the public light and with great acceptance. This is because the ancient wisdom teachings are now being transferred through the very path of soul initiation and from our personal day-to-day engagements.

In this day and age, the backdrop of initiation is daily life, as we gradually learn how to master the self from all separating responses, amidst our many unique challenges.

Initiation is also taken in sleep state. During our dreams, it is common for the soul to travel to many other dimensional frequencies. We often interact with other realities, etheric schoolrooms and even other versions of our self to learn and expand.

The requirements upon the path of initiation have changed quite a bit, keeping in pace with the planet's rising frequency and the sheer quickening of human evolution.

It was once said that the average person on Earth could awaken and experience self-realization within a span of multiple cycles of incarnations. Today, and due to the Earth's rising electromagnetic pulse, the opportunity for us to experience complete liberation has been exponentially quickened. We can potentially achieve full liberation in one lifetime.

Of course, many of us represent the starseed archetype and are great masters who came to the Earth to assist humanity's evolutionary shifts. For some of us, our greatest initiation is to just wake up and remember who we are and why we've come. We are already self-realized.

Even though there is a tremendous influx of supportive cosmic light that is saturating the planet, it is still entirely up to an individual's free will to raise the vibration and walk the path of initiation. Many people just are not ready to engage at this level of life experience.

In a lot of respect, it is much easier for those of us who are now on the path of spiritual development. This is due to the immense level of support available as a result of the mass awakening of humans all over the world. We have a plethora of resources, educational offerings, teachers and enlightened wayshowers who are currently gracing the planet.

This great awakening is now affecting the lives of countless millions of embodied souls who are all undergoing simultaneous soul initiation. This has created an ever-strengthening field of resonance and a new consensus reality.

Unlike in the past, we now have divine dispensation, which allows the granting of extra support and intervention from beyond the veil of physical reality. This includes a long list of multidimensional influences that are assisting Earth and humanity to evolve.

The planet's position in interstellar space is another major factor for accelerated soul initiation. The Earth is constantly moving, celestial events are occurring and we are experiencing tremendous surges of cosmic energy.

Much of this is streaming through our physical sun, which acts like a stepped down transformer to the high frequency universal light that is recoding and transforming our beloved planet.

We also have newly emergent planetary architecture to receive and channel this highly charged solar light, such as the Crystalline

Grid system. This is a term used to describe the emergent mor-phogenetic field and its matrix of high frequency energy.

Likened to a worldwide web of energy transfer, this unified grid field is helping to evolve the race from separation and conflict and into the non-polarized, timeless dimensions of universal principle, where totality and oneness are the reflection.

PHASES OF SOUL INITIATION

Please proceed to the next chapter to review the primary phases of human soul initiation.

"I am realizing my true self as an eternal and limitless being, one with Divine Presence."

PHASES OF
SOUL INITIATION

The profound changes we are all experiencing are essentially the result of Initiation's Path.

While change is the only real constant in our lives, the path of initiation has remained somewhat consistent to its original framework as the surest and safest method to attain full self-realization.

It has remained consistent because it is impossible to skip over any steps involved in initiation. Certain key areas must be brought under control and mastered prior to the expansion of the consciousness into higher realms of perception.

The one primary difference today is that we are swiftly transitioning into non-linear understanding. Our intuition is proving to be quite powerful and this is creating more independence from the constancy of left-brain, analytical thinking.

Another example is that our perception of time has loosened from its rigid hold and we are becoming more simultaneous and even timeless in our awareness.

Therefore, we are now experiencing certain phases of initiation as being fused and overlapping. It is common to experience initiation on many different levels and dimensions of awareness.

The following information is presented in chronological fashion to help you understand the phases of initiation that lead up to the embodiment of your Divine Presence.

This is a very brief overview of a very immense and boundless topic. It is shared to help you understand the colossal significance of your spiritual awakening and what phase of initiation you are currently addressing.

FIVE LEVELS OF HUMAN EVOLUTION

Generally, there are five primary levels of soul initiation that lead us into the self-actualized embodiment of Divine Presence. This is also known as the evolved human template of the new race genetic.

Each initiation represents a definitive stage of integration reached by the initiate and each of the main five is a synthesis of many smaller ones. We must move through all of the sub-levels to fully complete that particular initiation phase.

During the first three initiations, mastery of the three lower bodily vehicles is the primary focus so that the soul can make its transition into complete fusion with the human personality. This synthesis opens the doorway for deeper unification with its greater self-expression, also known as one's Divine Presence.

The meaning of the lower body vehicle is synonymous with the personality body. This includes the physical, emotional, mental and spiritual aspects of your make up.

Personal control over the physical body, the emotions and the mind must be attained and unwaveringly held before the further expansion into higher stages of consciousness can be safely permitted. In other words, advancement cannot happen until a certain level of balance and purification is attained.

This is where many initiates can potentially become disillusioned because it is imagined they are much further along than they really are. There is a tendency to fall into the trappings of other false realities especially when spiritual ego, emotional glamor and attachment to the self-identity are very much in play. This sets up scenarios of being caught in the nets of the ego and over zealous ambitions.

This is why the first three levels of initiation are in place, which is like taking a highly disciplined apprenticeship. It is a massive training to learn how to master the personality. This is the main preparatory stage into full embodiment of the Divine Presence.

Once we have passed through this training and enter into the fourth phase of soul initiation, we have nothing remaining as a so-called human attachment. This concerns the co-dependencies of the human personality including those bonds held by the physical senses, the emotions and the mind's belief systems.

The path of initiation is not taken by the human personality. Rather, it is the soul that is initiated. Each successive phase of initiation indicates that the soul has gained dominion over some aspect of the lower nature.

Once the lower nature is under control and attachment to all of its human identities is removed, the phase of soul fusion begins and takes us into true divine embodiment.

Our goal is achieved when, at the fifth phase of soul initiation, we stand as a liberated being, fully embodied as Divine Presence. We function as an omnipresent forcefield of intelligence from which to serve the human race.

Each of these five phases of soul initiation will now be reviewed in just a bit more detail.

FIRST INITIATION PHASE: CONTROL OVER THE PHYSICAL BODY

The human being is brought to the path of initiation by its own soul and often through self-contemplation. It is common for all of this to begin when the individual starts asking questions like, "who am I?"

As soon as a person questions the nature of reality, the inner divine seed sprouts and the great awakening begins. Through this inquiry, the soul aligns itself with its physical vehicle, the incarnated human.

This initial phase is commonly referred to as "the birth". The soul's energy starts influencing its human vessel. The resultant inspiration prompts the human personality to begin orienting itself to the spiritual side of life.

This beginning phase has everything to do with gaining personal control over the physical body and it sensory mechanism.

There is great need for the right amount of purification, which then allows the body to integrate higher levels of energy and light frequency, without harm to the physical body matrix. In a sense, the beginning phase on the initiatory path is like a built-in safety valve.

The neutralization of polarity to the physical senses is a great focus at this level. There is also great desire to alleviate personal suffering as one begins to make departure from its rather robotic life and the 'herd' instinct. The struggle to conform to the highest standard is experienced.

Out of control bodily desires and the resulting sensory attachments endure a thorough house cleaning.

The diet and lifestyle get cleaned up, compulsive behavior, addictions, and carnal desires are brought into moderation and regulated. The ego's control over the physical body is eventually tamed. The basics of the right living, thinking and self-control are successfully reached.

Some basic principles of God Consciousness begin to govern the person. The lower centers are motivated and impelled by higher impulses. The purity of loving motives and a spirit of goodwill are often demonstrated.

Generally, a more comprehensive and inclusive attitude to all beings is demonstrated.

As a result of control over the physical body, a great surge of creativity begins to manifest in one's reality.

SECOND INITIATION PHASE: CONTROL OVER THE EMOTIONAL BODY

The next deepening of the soul's initiation concerns personal control over the emotional responses.

The emotional construct is the most powerfully developed body of the human vessel. Balancing the emotional response is quite often the longest and most difficult of all of the initiation phases to bring into absolute harmony.

The death of desire from the controlling ego and its emotional glamour is one of the most important attainments of this initiatory phase. The lower nature experiences a rapid dissolve along with old attitudes, conditioned beliefs and desires.

There is a growing list of challenges, deep dissatisfaction with oneself, and often, an agonizing realization of seeming failure. There is a constant effort to clear and release emotional imbalances.

The way out of the muck and mire of emotion comes with a period of intense suffering, while so much of the held glamour, fantasies and false ideals are illuminated.

This is the phase of what many individuals experience as the "dark nights of the soul", where the death of negativity and negative desires ensue. The initiate, enmeshed in these traps, is required to free himself from the emotional bondage.

Emotional energies gradually stop controlling and impacting the initiate. Eventually, all that remains is a sensitive response to all forms of life and a passionate aspiration to be of service to others.

Freedom is the keynote of the individual who is facing emotional body initiation and its aftermath, all in preparation for the third phase.

THIRD INITIATION PHASE:
MENTAL CONTROL AND SOUL FUSION

Just as the fogs of emotional glamour have to be dissipated, the illusions of the mind must also be dissolved. This concerns the ability to control the egoic mind and releasing oneself from its held distortions.

As the human mind makes its shift, it becomes very responsive to ideas, intuition and impulses coming from soul awareness. The initiate begins to receive direct guidance from the soulful presence.

This is the phase of initiation characterized by constant perfecting and refining of the entire personality body and mastering the physical, emotional and mental faculties.

It is deep and very intense personal work that culminates into a great transfiguration of the human expression.

This is when the individual self-actualizes its truer identity as the soul, with soul powers, soul relationships and soul purpose.

By definition, the soul is the medium, or the middle principle, representing the relation between spirit and matter. It is the link between God and the human form.

The soul is that which provides consciousness, character and quality to all manifestations in form. It serves as the inner guide of the human personality.

It is now the soul that completely embraces and infuses the personality. The soul, itself, assumes the dominant position and not the egoic vehicle.

When the physical body is pure, the emotions stable and steady, and the mental body controlled, a person can safely wield and wisely use the higher sense faculties.

Emanating thought forms become clear and well defined. They are no longer controlled by the lower mind or emotional desire.

At this stage, the initiate is gaining more understanding of the principles of God Consciousness, while thinking in wider and more inclusive terms. There is growing identification with the soul, which is realized as the one soul of all humanity.

This shifting polarization to align with divine principle occurs because there is dwindling dependence upon the self identify, with its old habits and interests of the programmed societal matrix.

Working entirely with a neutralized posture, it is common to feel that one lives in the world but is not of it. Total commitment is maintained to the personal mission and to a life dedicated in service.

This third initiation is a high stage of evolution, yet it too can come with much pain, suffering, and sacrifice. The initiate is more accepting, though, knowing that the spiritual path is both the way of sacrifice and the way of inner peace.

FOURTH INITIATION PHASE:
MASTERY OF THE SPIRITUAL SELF
TRANSITION INTO UNITY CONSCIOUSNESS

The fourth phase of initiation can feel like a crucifixion due to the great levels of involved renunciation. This occurs as a result of one's preferred departure from the programmed human matrix and all of its emoting attachments.

It is at this phase of the great awakening that the initiate bears all and stands naked upon the altar of surrender to the greater Will. Direct contact is actualized between the transcended personality body and the Divine Presence.

The soulful personality becomes a direct instrument of service under the direction of the Divine Presence. The God force becomes the most prominent guide and teacher.

The initiate transitions into a brand new morphogenetic resonance, which dissipates all rhythms connected to the conditioned matrix of the human nature.

For example, the needy bonds of emotional love are transcended into divine love. There is no longer the tendency to blame, project and judge outwardly. It is realized that all creation and manifested realities lie within oneself.

Spiritual training is intensified, and the accumulation of knowledge is rapid. Multidimensional vision is developed. Oneness is directly experienced. The initiate can effectively command and wield the transforming cosmic light.

It is common to have the role of leading large group work, teaching many people, aiding simultaneously in many facets of humanity's evolutionary advancement.

Past experiences are discarded. The past has served its purpose, leaving one with masterful wisdom gleaned through direct experience.

It is very interesting to note…

The great being that is referred to as "Jesus the Christ" came into the world as a human disciple and third degree accomplished initiate.

He was not required to go through the first, second, or third initiations. He went directly into the assumption of the fourth initiation that is being shared about here. He went through it in full, physical embodiment.

This he did in order to dramatize the idea of renunciation and the significance of this phase of initiation, which relinquishes attachment to personal identification.

It is in the fourth phase of soul initiation that the initiate overcomes the physical world of matter. It no longer has any lure. Anything and everything can be given up, having died the death of the lower nature. The entire human life is renounced for the Divine Presence to fully embody the human form.

This all leads us to our fifth and final initiatory phase when the embodied Divine Presence is actualized, fully and completely.

FIFTH INITIATION PHASE:
MASTERY OVER THE MATERIAL REALITY
FULL UNION WITH THE DIVINE PRESENCE

The fifth phase of soul initiation is the emphasized goal for humanity's evolutionary leap.

This is the rising out of the pull of materiality and into a spiritualized consciousness. This is characterized by a new race genetic of Divine-Humans and liberated masters of creative, universal energy.

The fifth initiation is preparing the soul for the mastery over the world of matter. This means to have willful control of the pull of the material dimension and its façade of illusion.

This is the point in development when there is full embodied understanding of its image and likeness as Divine Presence, a direct aspect of the God force, containing all individualized, multidimensional expressions of the one evolving self. The experience is absolute oneness from the still point of being.

The initiate is essentially ascended and free, a master of the Earth plane. One has mastered the human program and its lower nature, triumphing over the conditioned response.

Moreover, the individual soul is free from karma because it no longer abides in the resonance or is in vibrational adherence to the code of linear time.

Such mastery of thought has been developed that the initiate no longer has negative desires. One is not even capable of having negative thoughts and all energy streaming from Absolute Source is consistently divinely qualified.

The initiate has spiritualized the body and its energy system and no longer needs to incarnate on the planetary body, except by choice, and to serve the ascension of the human race.

The individual is highly attuned and extra sensitive to a range of energies and influences due to the increasing polarization to the ever-expanding God force.

After the fifth initiation, the way of higher evolution is now a choice point regarding further levels of initiation to be taken. This refers to ascended mastery and the subsequent departure from the Earth plane.

*"I am thinking in wider and more
inclusive terms. The desire to serve is strong.
A greater creativeness has manifested within me.
The lower centers are motivated and
impelled by higher impulses."*

PERSONALITY TRANSFIGURATION & SOUL FUSION

O ne of the most influential initiations on the spiritual path, and one that marks a grand turning point in our self-transformation is referred to as soul fusion.

This is the phase of spiritual awakening when the human personality and the incarnated soul meld to become one unified entity. It is then that a refined and more soulful personality assumes the dominant position in life and is charged with a great sense of purpose.

It is the attachment to the personal human identity that is one of the most challenging to release. Societal programming continually plays upon who we are as a personality. It is how we are judged and even glorified in human culture.

Yet, our human personality is impermanent; therefore, it is not even real. It is made up of emotional, mental, physical and spiritual energies that are continually in flux and change.

Up until now, the channel of the personality has been a pathway for the soul's expression. Likewise, the soul has served as a pathway for the expression of the Divine Presence. Essentially, the soul has been in the middle, bridging messages from the greater self to the human personality.

After much purification of the personality, we finally reach a point of great clarity and inner stability. The personality body has become so mastered that the soul's role as an intermediary is no longer needed. A vibrational upgrade occurs in which the two become one.

This is what esoteric texts define as being a 'soul-infused personality'. This polished and more refined personality moves out in front. There is now direct contact with our Divine Presence with no more bridging required.

Fusion is the stage where we make permanent transition into a life of higher purpose, focused solely in unity consciousness. This stage is where it will no longer be possible for you to be drawn back into the lower frequencies of divisive programming and ego tendencies. If it does happen, it is only for brief moments in time.

PERSONALITY TRANSFIGURATION

Let's more deeply explore this idea of personality transfiguration and what it means in the context of today's shifting paradigm.

Transfiguration is a multi-layered process of purification through which our human personality fuses with the light of the soul.

The soul is who you are as core immortal essence. It existed before you were born and will continue to exist after you die. The soul, as an embodied expression, is the active principle of divine immanence, the unifying universal consciousness present right within us.

The soul plays the part of a medium between the human personality and the Divine Presence. It is the soul that ultimately transforms and transfigures the human form into its higher expression.

It is only at a certain stage in our spiritual development that the outward expression of the Divine Presence becomes active. This is when the physical, emotional and mental bodies are sufficiently balanced and stable enough to marry with the soul as one unified entity.

This is an immense statement because it involves bringing many areas into great stability. It means that we have freed ourselves from all attachment to personal and material identity. It means that we are living with an attitude of equanimity with all that is happening on the stage of life. In other words, we do not respond by taking sides and no longer get triggered into a divisive response.

Transfiguration of the personality is not even possible until we can perceive beyond the form and material expressions. We are not solely driven by the five human senses. Perceptions of duality no longer control us and we have deprogrammed from our conditioned belief system.

All of this high level balance and stabilization triggers an alchemical reaction of fusion and synthesis within our energy field. With determination to handle life solely from the angle of divine consciousness, and not from an emotionally driven response, we experience the transfiguration of our entire lower nature. Our self-attaching desires, feelings, pains, and pleasures shift into a greatly expanded mental focus.

We become intelligently motivated and can perceive beyond the form and experience beyond the window of the body-bound senses. As we carry out our service to life, we serve as a bridge between the matrices of consciousness, between the form and the formless.

During soul fusion, life ceases to be driven by material attachments. We are sincerely focused upon the realization of our oneness with humanity to which we have humbly dedicated our life in service.

The fusion of the personality and the soul arises out of deep spiritual attunement. Further, the free will of our personality is completely surrendered over to a greater Will, or, Divine Will. We now function from intentions that are firm and unshakeable.

This is the point of our training that we can offer ourselves up as a prepared vessel for the authentic embodiment of Divine Presence.

CLUES OF PERSONALITY-SOUL FUSION

In summary, soul fusion is a long phase of purification and preparedness of the human aspect, even for the most dedicated spiritual initiates.

Sometimes the personality's transfiguration phase can span several years, decades, a lifetime or lifetimes. It all depends on your purpose for incarnation and what you came to Earth to experience.

It can take much less time for those who are prepared and have the determination to self-master the human program. The focus of soul fusion is on the transfiguring personality as it shifts into an integrated and refined composure that exudes adept spiritual understanding and prowess.

There are many clues that the fusion of your personality and soul is well underway. Many were already previously shared and following are a few more to consider.

When phases of soul fusion occur, a new personality arises. You no longer place a priority on your human identity and there is no harsh judgment upon your physical appearance. You recognize your body form as a sacred temple that houses the omnipresence, the love and the grace of your Creator.

Your consciousness is clearly vibrating above the human senses. Bodily desires such as food, sexual impulses, drugs, addictions and other carnal desires do not control you. All human aversions are in moderation and regulated.

You have control over your mind and thought processes. You do not feel confused. Thought forms are clear and well defined. When undesirable thoughts arise, you recognize and remove them immediately.

You are not a fearful or worrisome person. You are not experiencing lack. There is no longer a sense of struggling or suffering. Your consciousness is rooted and grounded in love, wisdom and compassion. You regard everyone as your equal.

There is a great sense of responsibility to be of service to others. You are openhearted and generous. Generally, you feel liberated and peaceful.

An inclusive attitude is shown in your walk and your talk. As a result, you are more universally aware and working from the frequency of collective coherence through the faculties of intuition, spiritual telepathy and active intelligence.

A greater creativeness has manifested within you. Total commitment is with the realization of your oneness with humanity, to which you dedicate your life in service.

It is often after the personality's fusion with the soul that you unequivocally know yourself to be pure consciousness, experiencing life in a human body while radiating a force of light that greatly affects every person you meet.

Above all, you are driven by the idea that as you are raised up, all life is raised with you.

"The development of concentration through meditation trains my mind to hold itself focused and steady in the pure, clear spiritual light."

LIGHTING UP
EMOTIONAL GLAMOUR

Transfiguration is a phase of initiation in which the human personality is preparing for eventual consummation by the flames of the soul, resulting in one, very radiant conscious light expressing.

This has been similarly portrayed in the life of Jesus Christ, especially the experience in the desert when he underwent his final and most enduring temptations of the soul. It was after this time that he majestically appeared to his closest disciples on the Mount of Transfiguration as a most glorious revelation of divinity.

This story exemplifies the actual completion of this initiation of "the transfiguration". It was then that Jesus, the so called, "God-Man", began his outward mission as a world teacher.

Many classic ancient texts including the Yoga Sutras of Patanjali and the sacred teachings of the Masters of the Himalayas, detail step by step, the laws, methods and means of the soul's unfolding and describe it as "the science of union". Even though we may be doing it a bit differently in these times, these references gift us with highly valuable insight into our current initiatory undertakings.

The familiar analogy used is that we are like an onion, peeling off many layers of illusion that directly affect the ability to embody our greater light.

There comes a moment, however, when one is finally ready to enter through these initiatory gates. The foggy veil finally lifts, and, in clear view, the mesmerizing influences of life's current illusions are deeply realized.

This is often a most challenging time of humbling revelation. This is also a moment of tremendous rejoicing as it indicates the preparatory phases into an entirely new human expression and one's repolarization into the supreme mind.

Our current aim of development is to bring the desirous personality vehicle under complete control so that the soul-infused personality can be both the inner and outer light expressing.

No matter how devoted, sincere or the number of years on the Path of Initiation, most everyone has remaining personality aspects that are clothed in illusion, especially that of emotional glamour.

EMOTIONAL GLAMOUR DEFINED

Glamour is the result of a negative emotional focus. It is emotion driven desire colorizing itself on an illusory screen through the lens of the conditioned human personality.

These illusory forms enliven our lives, sometimes with ecstatic sensations. They also produce limiting consciousness patterns, which outplay in fantasized realities, false values, misleading desires, distorted perceptions and many needless necessities.

Some of the most tenacious emotions of glamour are so deeply embedded that they are not even recognized or thought of as hindrances to greater revelations in consciousness. The condition of glamour is an inherent component of our make-up stemming from ancient astral patterns and age-long personality desires.

For those of you who are in resonance to past histories and according to the writings of the Tibetan Master, Djwal Kul, the glamourized emotional body was brought to a high point in the Atlantean civilization many thousands of years ago. He quotes that much of this imprinting has been carried over into our current race.

Esoteric philosophies also attribute the world problem of glamour to the idea that the planet has been under the influence of great devotion and idealism during the last 2000 years. We can certainly understand why the world is in such turmoil from this one, exaggerated condition alone.

SPIRITUAL GLAMOUR AND DISCERNMENT

One of our greatest challenges in phases of personality transfiguration is to distinguish between authentic higher messaging versus that of astral psychism. This is one of the major prevailing factors that causes much delusion and misinterpretation among spiritual aspirants.

Astral psychism can be defined, in this context, as messaging derived from false, emotionally based substance. What we may intuit as divine messaging is oftentimes a glamourized reflection, which is always clothed with distortion.

This common and quite innocent type of misinterpretation comes as a result of one's polarization swinging more to the emotional nature versus being steady and centered in the light of the soul.

The quickening of incoming planetary energies and the resultant opening of our psychic nature has created a plethora of information and with many interpretations of, so called, "cosmic truth".

It is for this reason that continuous reflection and deep discernment are absolutely necessary to guard against misleading directions and the creation of emotion based fantasized realities.

It may also be appropriate to contemplate that many of the Masters and cosmic teachers communicating with us focus solely on an evolved soul level and higher mental plane. This is a frequency field of pure light intelligence versus the denser physical plane of emotion.

It has often been said that humans cannot make true direct contact nor be directly contacted by higher dimensional beings and guides if there remains personality limitations, including states of emotion and attachment to the individual self-identity.

Some of our claimed guidance, divine channelings and "messages from the Masters" are merely emotional reflections as a result of such discord. Examples include personal longings, spiritual pride, speculative belief, stored subconscious information and the tunings-in to mass mind concepts.

It is common to wonder if what you are receiving on the inner is either truth or fantasy. If you are ever in question, sincerely ask your Divine Presence to reflect the truth to these matters by clearly revealing any held illusion or false emotion.

Keep in mind that any activity associated with channeling outside energies is information that is being received and filtered through the veil of the human personality. If there are any existing personality limitations of the receiver, there is most assuredly a degree of discrepancy to the message.

There is no need to channel entities once the ability to intuitively receive from one's own illuminated consciousness and Divine Presence is developed.

As initiates on the spiritual path, we constantly endure phases of self-refinement to finally break through of the spells of illusion. May we continue to constantly question everything and with the great light of discernment applied to all information. This will ensure that we are not accepting a message as true just because it is beautifully or intelligently expressed. This is how false mass mind concepts are created and energized.

Indeed, the most effective method of discrimination is to develop the powers of pure reason and intuition through the illumination of one's own developed consciousness. Herein lies the real message of discernment.

IDENTIFYING AND DISSIPATING GLAMOUR

There are an infinite number of ways that emotions can be glamourized. These false formations can always be found where there is any degree of criticism, pride, emotional attachment, behaviors of separatism and a sense of superiority.

At the end of this writing is a summary of the more prevailing types of glamour that keep the personalities of spiritual aspirants in a cloud of emotional desire. Please review each of these and determine if there is anything remaining to shift or refine in your consciousness patterning.

It is much easier to clear a condition once it is identified and loosed from its foundation. The simplest way to identify this false formation is to "ask" for the held illusions of consciousness to be revealed.

Moreover, the effect of a well-developed illumined mind, in continual conscious communion with the Divine Presence, naturally dissolves these emotional conditionings. The development of concentration through meditation can train the mind to hold itself focused and steady in the light of divine inspiration.

One of the greatest spiritual teachers of our time, Paramahansa Yogananda's primary message in his influential teachings centered around meditation as the surest way to enter the "the Kingdom of God" within.

Meditation and concentration can help train the mind to penetrate the ultimate reality leading to illumined understanding. They also help balance one's polarization from the emotions into the higher mental body.

Relinquishing hold to the many ways that we keep ourselves identified to the formed human expression is an important part of the transition into soul fusion. We are encouraged to continually observe all of our emotional responses and especially the motive behind desire.

In daily life, and as the Buddha expressed so well, it is extremely beneficial to assume an attitude of the middle way. This is a neutralized posture, which displays equanimity and divine indifference to all that crosses our path, inwardly and outwardly.

Perhaps the most important encouragement of all is to continue building and strengthening an intimate relationship between you and your Divine Presence, the pure love aspect of your being.

In summary, when the physical body is pure and poised, when the emotional body is neutral and stable and when the mind faculty is steady and controlled, our human consciousness can then make its next evolutionary transition.

Our sensitivities and receptivity naturally expand to receive continual impressions from our Divine Presence and through the unmistakable wisdom of our own intuition.

Further, this process of transfiguration firmly establishes the true power of group influence while elevating the collective into a unified consciousness field, which accesses divine wisdom. It is this transition that optimizes the human potential to be used most effectively as an illumined consciousness in service to the whole.

The pure love of our soul and that of the supporting universal energy is not personalized. It is all consciousness that resides in the field of absolute wholeness. This is an energy field that exudes selflessness and selfless service to the whole. There is no self-reference. There is no seeking of recognition.

COMMON TYPES OF GLAMOUR OF THE SPIRITUAL PATH

Please explore each of these emoting patterns to determine where you can make important shifts.

THE GLAMOUR OF SELF-IDENTITY

This one glamour alone is the major trigger for all other types of glamour and creates the greatest separation between self and other, between the human and the divine.

This is attachment to the personal self identity and its physical expression including the bodily appearance, the personality, a held image, to emoting responses and with attachment to roles.

The emotion towards one's identity creates unending desires, cravings, fears, doubts, neurotic thoughts and a continuous wheel of large and small sufferings in all areas of life.

THE GLAMOUR OF POWER

This glamour is often unselfishly created during a time when one feels to be in great spiritual alignment while experiencing great openings and new abilities. There is emotional attachment to the sense of power that develops.

There is then a growing tendency to call attention to ourselves and to the mission that we are carrying out. There is a tendency to feel that our view is the best view.

THE GLAMOUR OF MATERIALITY

This is the attachment of emotion to outer forms and false appearances, which creates desire for needless material possessions. It is the false perception of values that ignores true spiritual principles and our forward movement into selflessness as a group consciousness.

The present world economic situation is a result of this particular glamour to which we all have contributed.

THE GLAMOUR OF DEVOTION

This is one of the strongest glamours among spiritual aspirants due to deep devotion and dedication to the path of self-realization.

The high level of devotion can innocently result in the formation of personal desires and glamourized ideals. There is great emotional attachment to a teaching, a concept, a vision, a view, a teacher, a Master, healing something, assisting the Earth, etc.

The glamour restricts the more expanded vision while closing us into a box of fantasy, personality longings, a long list of desires and to do's. While immersed in this glamour, it is impossible for divine messaging to be correctly interpreted or even to enter.

THE GLAMOUR OF PSYCHIC PERCEPTION

As a result of the quickening of planetary energies, many people are opening into the realm of extra sensory perception. This provides easier access to the colorful and inviting realm of the psychic world and the illusory astral plane.

One thinks the incoming visions and messages are divine truth when, in fact, they are clothed with distortion. This occurs due to spiritual pride, zealous ambition and emoting attachment to the self-identity and its perceived abilities.

THE GLAMOUR OF THE SPIRITUAL PATH AND THE GLAMOUR OF DESTINY

As a result of emotional attachment to one's path, this glamour produces high aspirations but limiting vision, selfish interpretations and self-centeredness. This is due to the individualized focus versus true realization of group consciousness.

This is also the attachment of emotion towards the belief that we are special and have important work to do in the world. There is much preoccupation with identity and an overemphasis of spiritual ambition. Fantasized realities and various identities are created.

THE GLAMOUR OF SENTIMENTALITY

This glamour attaches to the personalities of others. There is overemphasis of emotion placed upon a needed response from another in order to satisfy a desired level of personal comfort. There is emotional reaction to another's emotional response.

It is also the strong emotional desire to love and to be loved on the human level.

This one is definitely very challenging to overcome in phases of personality-soul fusion.

THE GLAMOUR OF SPECULATIVE BELIEF

This is the formation of held concepts, beliefs and resulting emotional patterns based upon the attachment to information that is not derived from one's own illuminated consciousness.

The glamour produces conditioned belief through the blind acceptance of information from someone else's principles, theories and assumptions or from messaging that is based on a guess, a possibility, a potential, a prophecy or ancient claim, etc.

THE GLAMOUR OF THE MESSIAH COMPLEX

This is attaching emotion to the role of being a savior and the illusion of having to take on the suffering of others.

This is a very common glamour experienced by teachers and healers.

THE GLAMOUR OF SELF IMPORTANCE

This glamour produces an overemphasis towards a sense of duty or responsibility. There is hurriedness, impatience and always something to do, create and plan.

Self-centered tendencies create continuous desires to share the opinion, the experience, the creativity, and the message. There is much self-reference and talk, "my project", "my vision", "my view", "my experience".

"I walk in equanimity. From this neutralized composure, I live life in the eternal now with an evenness of mind that is undisturbed and unattached to anything of the temporary world."

TRANSCENDING THE CODE
OF SEPARATION

DISSOLVING THE DUALITY WITHIN

The "Great Awakening" of mass consciousness is in full momentum. We are waking up from a deep slumber and remembering that there is something much more about our humanness than what the eyes can see.

This has spawned a spiritual renaissance that is returning us to the realization of the truer, greater self.

The grand enigma of this massive movement is that we already *are* self-realized. It is only the programming held within the consciousness that keeps us blinded to this truth. It is this tenacious imprinting that undergoes major metamorphosis to eventually return to a state of wholeness.

During this holy recalibration, it is inspiration's guiding hand that impulses us towards new potential, and a far greater human expression. This expressive potential, referred to as Divine Presence, becomes the embodied radiance.

When you know the self and the Divine Presence to be one, unified entity, every thought you think produces a vibration that coheres your energy. This level of coherence becomes the reflective mirror of your life experiences and accomplishments.

By sustaining the awareness upon this holy influence, spiritual energy around you intensifies and expands. Naturally, the whole body responds and begins upgrading its vibration to house higher intelligence. It completely shifts in resonance as the body vessel thinks differently, feels differently and acts differently.

A new level of integrity manifests internally. Bodily systems start working more harmoniously. Emotions and biorhythms cease extreme fluctuation. Health issues seem to resolve more quickly.

With expanding perception and bodily harmony, cell biology changes. A grand unlocking takes place at micro levels. This goes so far as to even stimulate dormant DNA encoding.

These are some of the indications that the process of 'human code upgrade' is well underway.

WHAT IS A CODE?

Generally, a code is characterized by a sequenced arrangement of data that gives instructions for how something is interpreted or expressed.

This can be easily understood when considering the way our computers read and store data. Code is what makes it possible for software programs to work. Code makes beautiful websites. The apps on your phone function through their own unique strings of coded information.

We can compare this to our body's genetics, which function through detailed encoding. This code expresses as the ordering of nucleotides in the DNA molecules, which carries the informative data for cellular activity. The genes inside the cell's nucleus are strung together in such a way that their coded sequence conveys our entire human expression, including what we inherit from our parents and ancestors.

This encoding is what makes up our human blueprint. We are a programmed expression as a result of our specific and unique code. To embody more of our human potential, the body must upgrade its code to sustain higher levels of conscious intelligence.

Let's ponder these relevant truths...

» We are spiritual beings having a human experience. For spiritual essence to materialize in a physical reality, it utilizes a series of coded sequences to form a body.

» As a spirit, we make our initial physical imprint in the cell nucleus, as DNA. As a human, we are merely a coded expression, a program.

» Leading scientists are proving that genes and DNA do not completely control our biology. They are discovering that DNA is also greatly influenced by signals coming from *outside* the cell. This includes the energetic messages emanating from our thoughts and beliefs.

» Therefore, our consciousness also contributes to code creation. We can potentially upshift our human encoding by shifting the consciousness in how we perceive and interpret information.

» Positive shifts of perception and new feeling states can trigger rearrangement of our code. Moreover, consistent and expanding consciousness shifts can stimulate and even push out the greater potential that is held within dormant encoding.

Our human DNA code is written in only four letters; A, C, T and G. Just as we are merely sequences of a four-letter code, the basis of life is also very simple. We change and transform all the time. We are constantly redefining ourselves. From every one of our consciousness shifts, we are literally changing our internal code.

This is why great emphasis is placed upon intention setting and the building of coherence with Divine Presence, as presented in the initial chapters of this book. When we cohere and align our intentions with our greater self, we can embody more of who we are as a totality, as both a human *and* a divine being of supreme intelligence.

This chapter shares many ideas on how to upgrade your human code by shifting your belief system. As you keep expanding the consciousness, deeper and swifter phases of transformation ensue.

Following are a few examples of what may occur in the transformative process. This is shared to emphasize the immensity of what you are doing as an ascending human.

PHASES OF HUMAN CODE UPGRADE

» Cell biology changes and the DNA sequencing rearranges.

» Your entire energetic field shifts as well as your harmonic resonance.

» New reflections come in to mirror this new vibration and your ability to perceive from a more evolved state of awareness.

» Mental clarity and life impeccability increase.

» Much fusion and synthesis occurs internally to link you up with the higher mind.

» The brain fires differently, and you are able to perceive from the bigger picture and with expanded perception.

» The pineal gland is highly stimulated. The intuitive faculty opens. Your other receiving channels become more fluent in translating information from your higher mind.

» The nervous system is constantly recalibrating.

» The heart center is constantly expanding.

» You are building new energetic circuitry to sustain a higher vibratory expression.

» You feel as if you are constantly receiving downloads of higher messaging.

» Extra sensory perceptions come online.

» Your body becomes like a walking library in its ability to energetically imprint and store information.

» The radiatory field of your human matrix expands. It serves as a transforming influence upon others.

CORE CODE UPGRADE

Phases of divine embodiment are propelled through a step-by-step consciousness shift. Our changing perceptions shift the DNA code. Eventually, and after so many shifts, we can reform ourselves into a brand new human design that houses higher frequencies of love and intelligence.

This all begins with changing how we think. You've heard this time and time again. It is breaking the mold in the way we've been trained to think.

The single most influential perception that encodes humanity into so much turmoil is the thinking that we are separate from each other. This belief, together with all of its related wounding, is what keeps humanity locked up inside a jailhouse of limitation.

We must step outside of the box and outside of the walls of divisive programming to perceive from unified awareness. This means to formulate perception from the absolute totality of being.

With many of us doing this at the same time, we gradually shift consensus reality.

The only way we can reveal this highly coherent consciousness is to transcend the human encodment by dissolving our patterns of separation. This is true human morphogenesis. Once the new perceptual foundation of unity consciousness is sustained, we morph into a new presence of being.

DISSOLVING THE DUALITY WITHIN

It is the mass consciousness program of duality that keeps the code of separation deeply entrenched in the human form. Duality is perhaps our greatest dilemma as a collective race. The sheer ignorance of our true nature keeps us revolving around a wheel of great suffering and conflict.

Duality is a false program of perception created through the human ego and continually fed by its fears. It is the duality within us that is in resistance to another aspect of itself, due to a mind-set that perceives from separation. This perception has become so severely distorted that it has built up energetic fortresses of defense to keep it securely in place.

Duality divides through perceptual judgments. From this percep-tion, self-attaching desires and opinions are formulated; all from the separated self, thus, perpetuating the matrix of separation into which we have been born. As long as we continue to feed the dualistic matrix, we can never transcend it, therefore, will forever experience conflict in our lives.

It's certainly not an easy program to master. The human blue-print is encoded to perceive from separation. Not only are we dealing with genetic predispositions and ancestral imprinting, we are also born with divided brain hemispheres, memory loss, gender division and very limited sensory capability, to name a few.

Our highly polarized emotional blueprint fuels the duality extremes that are dramatically outplaying in our world today. This emotion-driven mindset brings division to everything it touches. It's one thing or the other, black or white, good or bad, right or wrong,

To give clear examples of how duality operates, we can look at the idea of supremacy and racist ideologies. In duality, the view is that one person is above another. It discriminates and holds prejudice. Some people believe their cause is more worthy, more deserving than others. People compare themselves to others, judging themselves as being better or worse.

Duality programming creates an "us" versus "them" mentality. Consider how the two forces of good and evil are always warring against each other. In this view, there is a tendency to either attack or defend. This ideology has become so extreme that humans are convinced that they must constantly compete, fight and even kill each other to maintain their righteousness.

Clouds of confusion arise out of the many labels used to identify who we think we are such as race, gender, religion, nationality, economic worth and political agenda. These labels and many more only keep us pinned under an oppressive spell.

In truth, the source of all is Absolute Creator, the universality of all manifestation. This means that all pairs of opposites have the same foundation. Abundance and lack are from the same source. Light and dark are from the same source. While different in frequency, they live on the same polarity spectrum, are extreme manifestations of the exact same energy and are deeply interdependent upon the other at the human level.

Ponder the ideas surrounding the perceptions of what is good and what is evil. There certainly are varying degrees of opinion! These ideas stemming from human consciousness are gross perversions of the one and true unified reality. The ideas surrounding good and evil are really illusions enlivened by human perception. This can really boggle the mind!

Good and evil are not something inherent to the universe itself. The universe just *is*. It exists. It expresses as one unified and interconnected whole, bound through the principles of coherence and love's cohesion.

There is only one overarching power in the universe and this field of energy is omnipresent, pure divine love. To say this is not just a statement of adoration and praise to our Creator. It is a statement of principle. It is a statement of the great universal Law of One, of absolute unity.

There is no second power that can compete and war against this. Absolute means *absolute*. Creator, expressing as Divine Presence in the physical reality, exists everywhere. It exists in the good things and also what is perceived as being bad. It is up and down. It is on the right and the left. It is both light *and* the dark.

The idea that we are separate from one another is a false program. God dwells in us and we dwell within this magnificent creation field. We live and have our entire being inside the body of absolute perfection.

Contemplate this. We are breathing every single breath inside the awareness of this all-pervasive field, which influences every aspect of our lives and every twitch of our muscles. The Divine Presence of our individual being has never left us and we have never ever been separated from this abiding love.

Divine Presence is a flourishing force of energy, with an ever evolving and expanding nature. To embody this energy in and through our physical form, we must free the human perception from the dualistic influences of attraction and aversion.

It is easy to do this when we focus on the bigger picture instead of the conflicting dramas. It is helps considerably when we focus all of our thoughts, words and actions on the highest benefit of all, whether good, bad or indifferent.

Through this alignment, we are operating in coherence with the universe and we begin to live, perceive and create from the divine consciousness within.

If we truly experience from the eyes of divinity, in the sense that all is a part of the harmonious whole, then we do not create a conflicting pole; thus, no tipping of the dualistic scales occurs.

This, my friends, is a golden key. This perception gives us the ability to work in the deep and muddy trenches if we must, yet, not be affected by anything in the trench! This is because we are consciously aligned and vibrating in unison with the wholeness of life.

Many people are already making this monumental transition. It is accomplished through dedicated efforts to completely shift the perceptual awareness and one that thrives in resonance to a more supreme system of thought.

THE GOLDEN PATHWAYS TO TRANSCEND DUALITY

The duality program is an immense subject matter that has far ranging implications for its complete dissolution within the human mainframe. There are, however, a few really big areas that, if addressed with full commitment, will bring you sure-footed and steady on the golden path of transcendence.

PERCEIVE FROM WHOLENESS

One of the most important considerations of all is to understand who and what you are as a consciousness field and to do so at the very best of your ability. Even if this is not so clear for you, form a habit to look at your life from a bird's eye view; especially if you feel confused or stuck in some emotional patterns.

The habit of always regarding the bigger picture can be developed and practiced so that the consciousness remains attuned at all times to the truer nature of your being. You must be vigilant, however, to elevate yourself above the human condition and its divisive default. This is to learn, first, how to live truly as an observer and then to simply be the witness to all that is rising and falling.

While you are 'out there' and looking down upon your life, remember that there is only one consciousness. This omnipresent grace weaves your life and everyone else's as well. It does not take sides because it exists in everything. It is the active intelligence in all things that we see, breathe, feel, think, touch and consume.

Keep coming back to the point of singularity and to the realization that you are one with it all; not separated. Everything is here for a reason. The circumstances in our life are giving a perfect experience for the soul and its evolutionary advancement.

Rather than judge and separate when times get tough, choose a different response. Try viewing these experiences as purposeful and meaningful, knowing no opposite. If we truly perceive that all is synthesized as part of an integrated whole, we do not push towards a conflicting view.

Many people have the tendency to focus on what is wrong with something, wrong with their life, wrong with the world or what needs to be healed and fixed. Often, these thoughts come from dualistic perception and negative programming.

Rather than focusing on what you think you need to clear or heal, consider a different perspective. Maintain your focus only upon what you are doing, the bigger picture of your life.

In the absolute truth, all on the material place is one monumental outplay of divine orchestration. Ultimately, it is all about you and your experiences to evolve the soul. Keep yourself attuned at all times to this bigger picture and dedicate all activity to your highest preferred outcome.

As a result, you just might experience a manifested reality precisely as you imagined. You might also experience a much smoother process with it being effortlessly outlaid for you by an all-embracing higher power.

Rather than spending a lot of precious time on the emotional imbalances or limitations that seem to get in the way, hold unwavering alignment to your intended expansion into a vaster expression. This way, your awareness can more at ease, while remaining clear, stable and with integrity.

To transcend the duality program is to naturally bring fusion to our dividing tendencies. We transition away from the dual lens and learn how to perceive from the wholeness of life. Then, the 'code of separation' has an open pathway to evolve into its higher expression... as the 'code of unification'.

We do this simply by knowing, without any waiver of doubt, that all is one. We do this by consistently acknowledging and living the principle that all life is part of an interconnected whole. You are a representation of the whole, merely expressing in the physical reality as an individualized part.

Divinity does not fight anything; neither is it conflicted. It just *is*, accepting of all. We are made in this image and likeness. Keep returning to the realization that you are an extension of creation.

"I do not fight anything; neither am I conflicted. I just am, accepting of all."

You are within God and God is within you. You are one unified whole. The sum total of all of your thoughts, feelings and actions is the way that your Creator expresses itself through the unique gateway that is you, as its human vessel.

From the constancy of feeling that you are coherently connected, you can rise above the illusion of separateness and never dip into it ever again. You can function more effectively in the external world because your foundation is anchored from a purer awareness, which is emotionally free from things of a dualistic nature.

If you get caught up in the nets of duality, remember to return to these truths. Remember to return to the expanded perspective of your wholesome self.

WALK IN EQUANIMITY

It is extremely helpful to take on the poise of an unattached observer to what is happening all around you, while not allowing emotional reactions and quick outbursts to get the best of the situation.

Without the emotional triggers going off, you become indifferent to the arguments and prejudices that govern the lives of so many people.

Observing without attachment is to walk in equanimity. This means to remain poised and calm even when tempted by strong cravings or repulsed by perceived negativity.

Equanimity describes a complete openness to the experience, without being caught up in separating responses. It is a cultivated inner stability, which arises from a deep awareness and acceptance of what each moment is presenting.

Equanimity also reflects an evenness of mind that is undisturbed by anything of the temporary world. We are simply a witness without any attachment to the doing or to the accomplishment, to fluctuating states of emotion, even to overwhelming sentiment. All extremes are inwardly resolved and brought to a middle ground.

We become neutral. The duality of "sides" falls away as we cease to be for or against anything. It is through our understanding of human evolution that we can more easily accept everything just as it is while offering sincere love and compassion to all.

Equanimity helps us to navigate the choppy waters of the dualistic world with grace and ease. This posturing requires great discernment in what we choose to get involved in and how we engage. This especially concerns those external battles and noble causes that carry two different points of view.

Equanimity is our real nature. It is realized from the remembrance of the one consciousness at play in the weavings of our daily life.

The nature of life on the material plane is just a series of temporal reflections, always changing. From this understanding, we steadily make transition to living our life from the absolute reality. This is the unchanging, pure awareness of the vaster self.

In the absolute reality, there is only one consciousness. It exists in everything. To make contact with and directly experience this one supreme consciousness in all things helps us to grasp the true understanding of equanimity.

It is born from neutralized awareness. When we are in this neutralized awareness, we do not attach to the world; rather, we see the world for what it is, as a learning ground for consciousness. We can be in the world but not be swallowed up by its human characters and conflicted realities.

There is no longer a charging impulse to give a quick opinion. We can put the emoting self on pause and allow the space of stillness to be the initial qualifier.

It is interesting to contemplate how we respond to life, seemingly from on autopilot. Most of these responses arise out of how we have defined something. The definitions we really want to take a look at are the ones that are clothed with a judgment, separation or those that carry high emotional charge.

How many times do we qualify something as being negative or really horrible because of how it looks? Imagine what would happen if we did not automatically assign a degrading definition to something and remain neutral in a non-polarizing posture.

Physical reality is experienced through our definitions. If we always view something as bad or negative, this is guaranteed to be the experience we will always have.

Consider changing your definitions and giving new meanings to things that you have previously viewed as negative, or interpreted as being bad, wrong or just plain ugly. In doing so, a new reality may just manifest right before your eyes.

As the circumstance unfolds, it does not matter what it looks like or feels like; remain balanced in the calm neutrality of it all rather than immediately giving opinion to it, qualifying it one way or another. Just pause and allow these situations to percolate in the consciousness. Maintain your poise in equanimity and as the detached witness.

As challenging as this might be, especially in intense and stressful situations, keep practicing your ability to remain neutral rather than jumping to conclusions or immediately assigning a definitive meaning. *Respond by not responding.*

A major block that keeps us spiraling upon the duality wheel is the polarized perception that perceives from the charging emotions. Our fears, doubts and worldly attachments are some of the emotionally based programs that cause core internal conflict and keep us blinded to any other possible reality. We allow emotional judgment to direct our affairs, which keeps us feeling as though we are deeply separated from the unified field.

When your emotional triggers relax, everything else that is not of that poised and neutral frequency band will fall away. Harmony through conflict is achieved.

Choose neutrality as a lifestyle! Open yourself up to recognize how you are defining events and then shift those definitions that are branded by divisive thought. Remember, reality is the product of your strongest beliefs. If you perceive from duality, then your life will be steeped in duality.

Sustain your poise in equanimity by radiating kindness and compassion to all. These are gifts of the soul and meant to be freely given. It doesn't matter whether we know someone or not, whether we admire them, or if they are really different. We are simply recognizing another person's basic humanity and the one commonality to be free from suffering.

One of the greatest services that we can give to life is to walk in pure equanimity. This role serves as a bright beacon and neutral-izing pillar, while selflessly invoking divinity to all life upon our path. This is what it means, *"to be in this world, but not of it."*

With a more detached posture, we come to master the duality within us, in full acceptance of the divinity inherent in all things.

DISSOLVE THE SELF-IDENTITY

To resist the mesmeric power of mass consciousness and its destructive duality program, adamant determination to change our perceptions is necessary. It takes a strong mind to resist the divisive human culture, as well as an impassioned and faithful heart to give that mind over to a greater will.

This cannot happen if we continue to splinter off through sepa-rating identification. It is only through the total relinquishing of one's energetic investment in the self, as a personality, that we will stop feeding the illusion of the dualistic mind and its mate-rialistic world.

This subject matter of releasing the self-identity will be addressed in much more depth in the next chapter, Ending the Ego's Game.

In summary, transcending duality is a great challenge; yet one that can be overcome through the development of non-polar-izing perception. Our daily spiritual practice becomes one of constant observation and keen discernment in how we are qualifying both our talk and our walk.

It is easy to claim allegiance to unity consciousness. Ask yourself, though, if there is any place within you that still perceives through a divisive lens.

Are you strongly opinionated? Do you take sides while criticizing the other? Do you strand strong for or against something? Do you judge anyone or anything as being wrong or bad?

The Divine Presence dwells in you and you dwell within this magnificent creation field. You live and have your entire being inside the body of absolute perfection.

The Divine Presence has never left you and you have never been separated from this Presence. This is absolutely impossible.

These very statements are true for every other person on the planet.

Once you realize that you are a part of the whole, and, that you are also the whole containing many parts, then you will come to experience that it is through the whole that you will be supported, most easily and most effortlessly.

In other words, when you allow yourself to fully and freely flow, as your unique expression of the whole, then you can radiate that connective feeling outward. The unified field responds and bounces back many beautiful experiences of coherence and union.

Hence, the human code of separation transcends into the code of union.

"I am allowing the ego to relax and step aside so that another, more advanced intelligence can take the reins."

TRANSCENDING THE CODE OF SEPARATION, PART II

ENDING THE EGO'S GAME

The extreme polarization of the mind and the emotions has kept the human race constrained under the veils of illusion for millennia. This is perhaps the strongest trait of our human blueprint and its highly vulnerable divisive nature.

As the story has been written, the human race has undergone a very long and painful period of spiritual slumber until such a time that a divine dispensation could be given to support a quantum leap of human consciousness into a completely new blueprint of awareness.

This long awaited blessing seems to have finally arrived. From all walks of life, mass numbers of people are waking up and asking questions. They are demanding answers and requesting greater accountability from governments, corporations, media companies, financial and other institutions that maintain coercive strong hold over human behavior.

The driving force behind this great awakening is an indescribable energy that cannot be seen, intellectualized or physically touched. Some people attribute this to Earth's position in hyper-space and a resulting inflow of transforming cosmic light. Others say that it is the unmistakable unfolding of a well-orchestrated Divine Plan.

However we want to perceive the immense changes or what is causing them, we are clearly experiencing a vast quickening in consciousness from a seeming unstoppable flow of willful pur-pose and benevolent grace. We are evolving into a brand new vibrational harmonic.

As a result, we are witnessing unprecedented breakdown of falsely built foundations. At the same time, a new ecology is aris-ing of the pure hearted and integrous.

As the pure of heart, we are constantly recalibrating to a new center point within, amidst the swift changes without, each time enlivening our inherent knowing. Our polarity is shifting, and, as a result, the hidden chamber of the subconscious reveals.

It seems that everything that carries a "divide and conquer" atti-tude is being overturned and ultimately transformed. We, our-selves, may feel constantly prompted to turn inwards to heal our own tendencies to run away and separate.

As we shift into a new, more balanced form of transparency, the layers of our pre-programmed, electrical-based sheath continue to unplug, to eventually unveil our illumined core.

Transforming this densely polarized, more electrical nature of our make-up is not an easy one to endure. It requires recalibra-tion our entire energy field while surrendering the very thing that has given us a sense of security, our dominating ego complex.

It requires great courage to stand naked in front of the mirror while habits, limiting thoughts, false perceptions and our con-trolling ways are revealed. This takes willful surrender of any pride and the humility of heart to go fully inside the transform-ing chrysalis.

Those of us choosing to make this grand shift, from separated thinking to unified awareness, must be ready to engage in a very dynamic, metamorphic lifestyle. We are doing this together, however, each of us alone must take the crucial steps in dropping all resistance and offering up, completely, the controlling ego complex and its electrical overwhelm.

Once the surrender happens, a grand and holy recalibration begins.

EGO TRANSCENDENCE

The main theme of this book is about embodying your Divine Presence and greater self-expression. You are not leaving physical reality. You are not kissing your human senses goodbye. You are not even annihilating the ego. This all is quite the contrary.

The transition you are making is into a fused blueprint and your greater potential as a Divine-Human. In other words, you are learning how to thrive as a divinely inspired human expression. This is a rich inner experience, which reflects as holistic integrity and absolute wholeness.

As you advance into this higher potential, the human self remains, as do its emotions, the ego and the five human senses. The difference is that you now get to play in in a whole new way. This mode is more inclusive and more expansive. You can operate within a multitude of frequencies and dimensions of vibration.

This new game is about freedom, and your ultimate liberation from human suffering.

It is your current system of belief that dissolves in this next phase of the consciousness shift. You are removing the fear driven perceptions and the electrically charged responses exerted by the ego and its drive to be the controller over thought.

It is this need to be 'in control' that dissolves as you shift into a more supreme thought structure, *as one with your Divine Presence.*

WHAT IS THE EGO?

In the context of divine embodiment, our human ego can be defined as that self-conscious aspect of the human personality that is identified as "I". In its possessive form, it is the "my" of our story.

Your ego makes contact with the external world through perception. It is that part of you that perceives itself as being separated from everything else. Because of this perception, it constantly competes with your spirit for control over the inner voice.

The drive of the controlling ego forces its way through life. This sets up a sense of internal pressure within the body make-up. This pressure gets in the way with our more preferred experiences of inner peace, harmony and deeply meaningful moments.

The ego thrives off of being in the driver's seat. It is absorbed with its survival and is quite adamant about protecting its identity, reputation, and personal interests. It's that part of us that seeks approval. It is desperate to be right. It always needs more.

It either doesn't feel good enough or it feels superior. The ego's actions inevitably lead to uncontrolled emotion, drama, conflict, stress and overwhelm.

The exerted dominance of the ego is difficult to see, because it hides behind opinions that appear to be true. These masks of belief are created primarily through its attachment to the many ways it identifies to the self.

The ego is very clever in its many manipulating subtleties. These can even be buried deep into our subconscious programming. The ego wants to make sense of things and will create realities to serve the righteous self.

It builds concepts upon concepts that turn into desires, attachments, justifications, frustrations, excuses and avoidances. The ego makes decisions based upon what feels comfortable and secure.

Do we need the ego? Of course we do! Ego is a necessary component of human life. It informs us of our choices in the world. It gives us our colorful sense of self, our boundaries, and a feeling of being *me*. Ego gives us personal definition in the matter dense world. It certainly can be used in many positive ways to help us carry out many day-to-day functions in a busy and fast-paced world.

Yet, we don't want the ego to be the main driver of our decision-making. By definition, the ego is limiting because is keeps itself isolated and self-serving. Its understanding doesn't reach beyond the physical world. Therefore, its scope of responsibility becomes even more limited as we advance into multidimensional living.

We have spent years building our ego-based self-images, living inside these images, and reinforcing them. Extracting our genuine self out of this matrix of false beliefs takes some time.

EGO TRANSFORMATION

The transformation of the ego and its dominating control over our emoting responses is considered a major capstone of our concerted efforts on the path of spiritual initiation.

It is only at a certain stage in our development that the outward expression of the Divine Presence becomes active. This is when the physical body, the emotional body and the egoic body are sufficiently balanced and stable to synthesize as one.

A more integrated personality is the result and one that becomes fully responsive to the inflowing energy of the Divine Presence. This increased receptivity to the 'greater' happens when we think in wider and more inclusive terms.

Our Divine Presence experiences reality in an entirely different manner than our human ego-driven personality. It is fully aware of all other dimensions, timelines, potentials and probabilities. Our ego self does not have this awareness.

To fully embody our expressive potential, it is imperative that we allow the death and dissolution of the ego's hold to happen. Whatever it takes to forever dissolve the monkey mind and the control of the free will.

Of course it is much easier said than done. The ego is a master of resistance. There are, however, many ways to tame the shrew. Following are some primary areas to help you rise above the ego's hold.

SURRENDER TO DIVINE WILL

Keep surrendering to the greater Will influence in your life. This greater Will, or Divine Will, is the driving consciousness behind all creation, a determined field of energy that penetrates through to the core of all things.

It is of unprecedented benefit to consciously merge with the greater Will, so that this holy determination becomes the pure mirror of our thought energy. When our desires are set forth in this way, each intention is qualified by the propelling force of love's intelligence.

As we come to recognize Divine Will as the guiding principle of our entire existence, we graciously surrender all attachment to the limited workings of the ego's will. We humbly realize that of our own selves we can do nothing, it is the Divine Presence within that does the work.

Calling Divine Will to you creates an enormous infusion of spiritual energy into your life that supersedes the will of the ego and awakens new realizations.

In working with Divine Will, any sense of pride or self-glorification must be released. Further, you must summon from the depths of your being an unwavering willingness to release all that you know is true.

This subject matter will be discussed in much detail in a forthcoming chapter.

NEUTRALIZE ELECTRICAL OVERCHARGE

Another way that you can neutralize the ego's controlling response is to look for any area of your life that is in electrical overload.

Our current societal scene is one that fuels an overcharged electrical frequency. For many of us, our attention is constantly with technology as we play, work, relate, and even sleep while constantly being plugged in.

We have created a societal matrix that is disconnecting from the magnetics of nature. This causes huge fracturing in our human energy field, thus perpetuating the electrical egoic response.

In addition, the fears that we hold plus other types of unbalanced emotional patterns keep us vibrating more electrically rather than from the more sensitive, magnetic qualities.

When we are magnetic, we are surrounding ourselves with love, the great universal power of attraction. With this, you are naturally invincible and irresistible. Positive magnetism is a very high frequency that always overcomes denser vibrations.

Mastering our ego and overcoming our forcing electrical current is very important to divine embodiment. This mastering of energy beautifully results in greater levels of magnetism and a loving radiance that naturally shines through us, affecting our entire sphere of influence.

Following is a list of examples illustrating how you might be electrically overcharged and some of the common areas that indicate a triggered ego response.

You probably have already addressed many of these, yet, do review them and see if you have anything remaining that can be worked on. Many of these are habits that go unnoticed or might be conditioned patterns that have been stuffed deeply down within you.

Are you electrically overcharged? Is your ego still out in front?

See if any of these apply to you.

COMMON EGO RESPONSES:

TERRITORIAL

» Driven by having a sense of personal territory
» Holding energy regarding 'what is mine versus what is yours'
» Always keeping secrets or telling secrets
» Having the constant fear of being robbed, over insuring
» Extreme focus on wanting, having, needing, owning
» Life is judged by what you own or the money you have

CONTROLLING OR BEING CONTROLLED

» Needing to be in control
» Engaging in subtle mind manipulations to get people to believe or agree with you
» Being controlled through external dependencies
» Dependence upon external tools and techniques to access supposed power (ie: cards, psychic readings, horoscopes, symbols)

» Being controlled through attachments to materialism or people

» Controlled by your fears and anxieties

» Controlled by sensual pleasures

» Controlled by money

» Controlled by a glamour of self-importance

» Controlled by societal programming

COMPULSIVE, OBSESSIVE, AGGRESSIVE

» Compulsive behavior and reactions

» Acts of oppression, obsession and aggression

» Acts of conflict, division, separation

» Needing to have a rational, logical plan, without waiver

» Resistance to breaking structure and routine

» Addiction to anything

STRONG EMOTIONAL POLARITY

» Quick emotional reaction without thinking or feeling things through

» Being antagonistic, argumentative, needing to feel right

» Defending, justifying, taking sides

» Seeing something as right or wrong

» Holding an attitude of 'us against them'

» Racism even on the subtlest levels

» Emotional states like fear, guilt, anger, resentment, and frustration

IDENTITY ATTACHMENT

» Always concerned about your reputation

» Worry about what others will think

» Fear of losing your identity

» Addicted to social media

FEAR, WORRY, VICTIM CONSCIOUSNESS

» Constantly scanning for threats

» Constantly thinking about your mortality

» Worry about what *could* happen

» Resistance to letting go of your belief systems

» Having a very structured life

» Not taking personal responsibility for the creation of your life experiences

» Blaming outside influences

» All forms of victim consciousness

RELEASING ATTACHMENT TO THE SELF-IDENTITY

As spiritual aspirants, we are on a dedicated path of mastering our personalities. This is overcoming all human condition and limitation that binds us to the perception of separation and the program of duality.

In this mastery of the small self, we are focusing on the realization of the true self as an eternal and limitless creator being, one with Source, as Source. Our focus is now authentically shifting from the personality "me" or "I" to the Divine Presence.

As we advance into expanded awareness, we can now safely leave the masked facades that have served us well yet now express as great distortion in our field.

> » We are letting go of all attachment to self-identity and perceived self-importance.

> » We are dissolving all notions of who we think we are and where we think we are from.

> » We are no longer focusing on our identity to supposed past lives, parallel lives, future lives and our dimensional selves.

> » We are dropping identity and attachment to any supposed mission to save the planet or to heal humanity.

> » With our inner awareness as the only guide, we are letting go of the need to confirm our identity and forward movements through external resources.

> » We are severing the cords to everything that binds us in attachment to our self-identity and that which directs us away from understanding the Greater Self as pure awareness, always present.

Sri Ramana Maharshi, one of the greatest spiritual teachers of modern-day India, devoted his entire life and mission to this one area alone. He stated that the sole cause of all human suffering is a false belief about who and what you are. For Ramana, there is no "true self" from whom you are separated, there is only you, just as you are.

He taught that the aim of spiritual development is to reach the root of the "I"-sense. Ramana stated, "To attain natural happiness, one must know oneself." He guided numerous aspirants into the primary practice of self-inquiry by constantly pondering upon the question, "who am I?" He said there could be satisfaction only when you reach the Source; otherwise there will be restlessness.

He believed the inquiry upon "who am I?" is the principal means to the removal of all misery and the attainment of the supreme bliss. He said the constancy of this method easily destroys egoity. Ramana focused his followers into the practices of devotion, meditation and concentration.

Just by taking an interest in this subject matter, you are initiating the dissolution of the personality's self-identification in order for the greater self to be unveiled in greater influence.

In truth, all that we really know is that we are here, now. All the rest is story. Self-inquiry assists us to see the truth of who and what we are now in this present moment. It is placing conscious attention to the simple, single knowing of our "hereness" for no other purpose than to see it and experience it directly.

In the absolute sense, we are *already* self-realized, liberated and free. We are only covered up in the layers of maya that prevent us from this simple understanding. We are masking our greater self through attachment to the dualistic world and who we think we are on this plane of illusion.

There is nothing external that can bring us into self-realization. There is no practice that we can undertake that will remove our false beliefs, apart from directly seeing the truth of our true nature directly for ourselves. There is no teaching, teacher, class or book that can reveal the truth of what we really are.

Teachers and other means of support serve to simply guide and inspire, however, the bottom line is that we each must do the direct "realizing" for ourselves.

Self-inquiry is one of the most important activities during these accelerating cycles of purification and dissolution. We can greatly benefit from constant and rhythmic focus placed upon deeper self-reflection, self-examination and self-contemplation as we continually call forth the deeper understanding of our true nature.

In our transcendence from the dual plane, the mind is being retrained to serve as a follower and not the leader. We are allowing the ego to relax and step aside so that another, more advanced intelligence can take the reins.

This takes focused surrender with constant reorientation to the heart. This foregoes the need to see things from the logic behind outplay. When the mind stays in the heart, the names, the forms, the stories and even the personality begin to disappear. With the mind naturally resting in the heart, the "I" dissolves and the greater self emerges.

When attachment to the self-identity dissolves, so do the ideas that you must constantly clear and clear yourself, heal yourself or activate your self. You release sabotaging patterns relating to the issues of low self worth, ego control, lack and victimization; the whole gamut of duality consciousness and its many masks.

Once attachment to the self-identity is truly surrendered, the human aspect can undergo greater metamorphic phases to actualize a fused template of a Divine-Human expression. The resulting vibrational upgrade moves us into a highly sustainable resonance, which enables us to perceive from, and be supported by the whole.

It is not an easy task to transcend the ego's hold to the material world. It has been said that this phase of the becoming is one of the most challenging of all, and, in past accounts, taking many lifetimes to accomplish.

It requires strength of will, steadfast determination, self-discipline and a constant reorientation of the mind so that the personality self can be held steady and true in the light of Divine Presence.

This is a vast subject matter and only briefly touched upon here to initiate greater awareness of your current undertakings.

There are many effective practices and disciplines for dispelling these hindering false formations of consciousness.

Many aspirants choose to develop the mind powers through disciplined meditation and concentration. There is nothing in the human or even in the super human field to which the power of concentration is not the key to the expansion of consciousness.

Certain yogic meditative practices are highly effective in taming the controlling ego. For example, Raja Yoga is a form of Hindu yoga intended to achieve control over the mind and emotions. It helps the devotee develop the right use of the mind as an instrument of the divine.

There are also many teachers who offer the studies of Advaita Vendata, a Sanskrit word meaning non-duality. This is one of the classic paths to spiritual realization. Advaita teachings believe that Brahman (Divine Presence) is the one and only reality and everything else is a mere appearance, projection or illusion.

Similar to what is presented in this book, the Advaita teachings of non-duality state that that the individual self has no separate existence of its own and is a mere projection or reflection of

Brahman (Divine Presence). We are only deluded by egoism, desires, and other impurities, and thereby, seemingly disconnected through our experiences of duality and separation.

Much of the subject matter in this book will greatly support your ego transformation, especially the chapters:

» Transcending the Code of Separation

» Repolarizing to Divine Mind

» Merging with Divine Will

» Transitioning into a new Thought Structure

The core essence of "Coming Home to Divine Presence" brings a grounded and practical approach to divine embodiment.

Really put your all into this melding! By placing all of your attention to be consciously merged with your Divine Presence, the illusion of separated identity can easily fade away.

Always remember… what you consistently focus upon eventually becomes your reality.

THE BIGGER PICTURE

It is during our own phases of self-actualization that we can better understand the true state of world condition, which is heavily clothed in a facade of electrical overcharge and egoic illusion. This has resulted in some very serious states of mass scale suffering.

The ultimate synthesis of the human ego into the illumination of Divine Presence is the only real way that we are able to most effectively offer service to others who are also undergoing the consciousness shift.

The true spiritual leaders and teachers of wisdom are emerging in greater numbers to help guide humanity across the bridge and into the new consciousness reality. These are common people from every race, religion, nation and culture who have liberated the self from identity attachment and the ego's fears.

With divine indifference and deep inner peace, these light bearers stand humbly at their center. They radiate compassion and selfless aspiration to simply serve as an extension of the whole.

They are without self-reference. They are without needless chattering. There is neither coveting nor personal claim of ownership to their creative presentations of truth.

There is only emanating love and great wisdom as a result of the realization that all comes from universal mind and the field of one.

"I am shifting my mind's default by consistently placing my focus upon the greater, and with the highest version of who I really am. This Divine Presence is the one and only navigator of my life."

BREAKING THE BONDS OF
HABITUAL THOUGHT

An invincible lock that prevents intimate communion with our Divine Presence is unserving habitual thinking. Nothing does more to hold us back than the looping patterns of stale thought forms that consistently reflect a same old predictable life.

Lower frequency thoughts and patterns that are still rooted within the inner landscape obscure the reality that we really prefer to experience. We must exercise our vigilance to shift beyond our own habits of lower density thinking and completely embrace a new structure of thought.

Often, our habits can be so ingrained in everyday life that we are not even aware of them. It is this habitual way of believing, thinking and acting that you are encouraged to look at more deeply.

When it comes down to the way we think, it always defaults to the memorized pathway that we have always thought about something. As soon as we think a thought, the energy of that thought goes out and immediately begins coalescing into a manifested physical response.

Therefore, we have to catch ourselves in the action of a non-serving thought, cancel its projection and then create a new and more preferred pathway for the thought to travel... right there on the spot!

If you have already sent out an unserving thought and recognize your action, immediately call it back to you and cancel it with your determination. Then, re-qualify it with a new and more positive one.

As you practice this, pretty soon you will catch yourself during the act of the thought. With more practice, you will catch yourself just before the thought has even formulated. Finally, the unserving pattern of thought will have dissipated for good.

It is so easy to declare our new and evolved perceptions outright, but when we are busy living life, we think and do things out of habit. Often, these habits take us out of congruence with our truth and what is for our highest good.

Observe your thinking and the resultant behaviors that are on autopilot. Take some quality time to contemplate how you are defining your life, including relationships and experiences.

Are you giving any of this a negative interpretation? Are your definitions invalidating the self in any way? Where can shifts in your thinking be made to reflect a different outcome?

Dissect your thinking, thought by thought, as a way to uncover the little trolls that want to keep you bound up on the wheel of limitation. When you discover a limiting definition, reformulate it into a meaning that is aligned to the preferred reality that you desire to create.

THE EXAMPLE OF LACK

For example, one definition that is prevalent within many people concerns "lack" consciousness. It is very common to constantly affirm that there is not enough. There is not enough time, there is not enough money, not enough help, not enough love, not enough peace, and so on.

This also relates to the "more" syndrome. I need more of this, more of that... more clothes, more food, more minutes, more, more, more.

Why is there constant affirmation of the belief that there is not enough? A lot of times, it really just boils down to the memory field and the false imprint of lack. Lack operates at the most subtle layers of our consciousness and we do not even realize it.

Often it is through the use of our words alone that we get clothed in limitation. We can release habitual thinking just by changing the way we talk and use our words.

Regarding lack, one way to shift out of its patterning, is to make a shift in the thought structure. Consider the idea that your Divine Presence is the God power. It governs all manifestation in your life perfectly. It is the power producing it and the force sustaining it.

To embody the Divine Presence is to have complete reliance upon that which moves in the deepest side of your nature and what is referred to as, the God within. When you stand unified with this divine principle, all is magnetized to you in spontaneous flow, in perfect timing and in just the right quantity.

No strenuous effort is required. No affirmations are needed. Even the idea of prayer becomes obsolete. "Want" and "need" become signals to what is already in manifesting motion.

THE EXAMPLE OF IDENTIFYING WITH THE PAST

Another big definition that can be rejuvenated and one that binds us to heavy vibrational density is the constant adherence to the past and living according to what once was, or, how it has always been done.

If we continue to code our reality from what once happened, this takes energy away from the presence and the alchemy of "now". Consider that no more processing of the past is even required. You do not need to clear and clear and clear all these past hurts and traumas anymore.

You are moving into a brand new thought structure that is changing the entire person that you are. To heal the past is old paradigm. Just let those images, that past association of you go. You are a child of God that lives constantly in a field of grace. How can anything be imperfect? Life is merely a series of experiences.

There is no need to look back. The old you does not even exist. You are always in the process of becoming something new. You are always manifesting the self as a new idea.

Just keep growing forward, constantly defining and redefining what is it that you prefer with clear intention, clear action and always validating yourself. This will re-pattern your energy and vibrational resonance very quickly.

One of the very best ways to rise out of limitation is to always remember your current reality is a mirror to what is going on inside of you. Your current reality has manifested as a result of your innermost dominant thoughts.

Practice shifting your mind's default by consistently placing your focus upon the greater, with the highest version of who you really are. Then, allow that greater self, your Divine Presence, to be the one and only navigator of your life.

When you know the Divine Presence to be your master driver, your intentions can be accomplished more quickly. It is from this state of knowing, that every question is answered and every thought that you think produces a vibration that coheres your energy.

The divine reality exists within you and around you at all times. You only have to drop the conditioned human thoughts to allow the expansiveness of eternity to reveal the guidance from divine grace, present in every moment.

To know this grace is to know and experience the Divine Presence manifesting in your life. As a result, this becomes the pure mirror of your thought energy.

There is no greater mirror in life than this.

"I know the Divine Presence is acting through me in every moment. This master thought increases my willpower and the ability to accomplish as the pure, illuminating spirit of all life."

MERGING WITH
DIVINE WILL

The initiation of personality transfiguration and eventual soul fusion is quite possibly one of the longest and most enduring phases upon the path of self-realization.

What seems to make this long trodden passage of purification go more quickly is when we surrender all that we think we know to the Divine Presence, and the greater will aspect of our nature.

What is it meant by the greater will?

Behind all of universal creation is an immanent force of energy that administers it, an invincible energy of Divine Will, a powerful electrical force of pure spiritual energy.

Divine Will is the driving consciousness behind all creation and is responsible for the great spiritual awakening in our evolving world. It is this living forcefield of guiding energy that holds the planet and all upon it in one coherent manifesting whole.

Divine Will works out the evolutionary plan. It penetrates through to the core of all things, guiding the evolution of the human intelligence. Calling it into your life creates an enormous infusion of spiritual energy that awakens and illuminates the consciousness.

In setting intentions for your life, a very powerful objective is to have all of your will in complete focus with the Divine Presence so that your personal will merges with the greater will. Then, this becomes the pure mirror of your thought energy.

As we come to recognize Divine Will as the guiding principle of our entire existence, it is much easier to graciously surrender all attachment to the limited workings of the personality's will. We humbly realize that of our own selves we can do nothing, it is the Divine Presence that orchestrates it all.

A personality that is fused with the greater will provides the neutralizing antidote to its opposing shadow; the tenacious will of the ego to divide and separate. This synthesis results in a crystal clear intention coupled with sincere determination; an attitude that never gives up until we know that our life purpose is fulfilled.

LIVING THE LIFE DIVINE

One of the greatest services that we can give to our evolving race is to see the perfection of the Divine Presence in everything.

When the thought of the Divine is held while carrying out our daily life activities, this supreme energy percolates into our personality. It starts expressing in our actions, feelings, and speech.

This is the manifestation of the common expressions, "bringing Heaven to Earth". The Divine is entering from the most expanded planes of consciousness to express through us in daily life.

This evolved perception, where there is no judgment or separation, is the ascending consciousness. This is a dimensional consciousness shift that takes us into a completely new way of living and perceiving. It is as simple as this; we are seeing, feeling and being as the Divine Presence in our daily lives, *always*. Our synthesis with this greater will momentum gives us incredible ability to magnetize and to accomplish as one with the pure, illuminating spirit of all life.

We make full passage into this state when we have mastered the human personality, transforming all the ways that it behaves as a separated entity, both in perception and outward activity.

We cannot evolve our consciousness to this advanced level until the human attachments and unnecessary distractions in our lives are replaced with a sincere, altruistic motive.

Therefore, and to make this really simple, it seems that we have one main objective to accomplish. This is to have all of our personal will merged with the greater will, so that this sacred marriage becomes the reflective mirror of our thought creations.

When our desires are set forth in this way, each intention is qualified by the propelling force of love's intelligence. This fusion of Divine Will then empowers an indescribable invincibility in any direction that we desire to go personally and collectively.

Consciously drawing Divine Will into your life can:

» unfold your highest potential

» expand your consciousness

» assist you to manifest in accordance with your divine purpose

» open your vision, deepen your intuition, and release limitations

» liberate your spirit from the bonds of matter

Divine Will infuses your personality with new skills and more power to carry out your soul's goals and purposes. Working in this way can create profound changes in your life.

You can totally transform your life by consciously aligning to Divine Will. Even if you don't yet understand it from an experiential perspective, just start calling it towards you, with a fully open heart and receiving mind.

It is really important to have a sincere conversation with your ego. Let it know that its job has been greatly appreciated but now it is time for it to simply rest in peace. Let it firmly know it can relax now, but in the back seat!

Once your ego is tamed, the invincible and unfailing greater will can override your human operating system.

PERSONAL DESIRE VERSUS DIVINE WILL

Desire comes from the will of your personality. It is a driving energy that arises from the personal ego. Divine Will influences us from the unseen realms of light and travels multidimensionally, transforming every level of your being and all the energies it contacts.

You may call Divine Will into your life to assist you in fulfilling a particular desire. When it comes to you, however, Divine Will supersedes the will of the personality. It may or may not fulfill that desire, and that is perfectly okay.

Divine Will simply becomes your will and your inner promptings start reflecting your highest purpose and the divine plan for your life.

As you draw in Divine Will, it becomes easier and easier to know what you need to do. Divine Will comes with its supportive streams of energy to assist you in carrying out the actions that seem indicated.

Do not expect that you will be "taken over" by Divine Will and that suddenly everything will work in your life without your needing to do anything. You are still living on a planet of free will and are learning how to choose and discern for your higher good.

You are the one who must take action and carry out the inner directions that are emerging.

Have some form of regular spiritual practice that helps to keep you aligned to this idea of the "greater you" and the current of Divine Will, which is really the one and only orchestrator of your life.

Formally surrender your personality's will. Then, constantly affirm that your will is Divine Will.

Know that the Divine Presence is acting through you in every moment. This master thought increases your willpower and therefore your ability to accomplish as the pure, manifesting presence of life.

A VISION FOR PLANETARY PEACE

The Divine Presence is the manifestation of everything that is considered good, just and whole. It is through the influence of supreme benevolence that all things exist and evolve.

It is the outer reflection of this benevolent will on our planet that brings about the ultimate demonstration of coherent human relations. The agent and reflection of Divine Will on Earth is the global manifestation of goodwill towards all life.

In fundamental simplicity, it is the outpouring of goodwill that catalyzes a greater consciousness shift en masse to potentially birth an era of lasting global peace.

As the agent of Divine Will, goodwill creates a pathway between more evolved spiritual realities and human life, and builds an expanding channel for the inflow of transformative, subtle energies.

This, when truly established and radiated by greater numbers of people, is the required preliminary agent to actuating the cascading effect of worldwide spiritual revelation. All people may finally realize the need to rise up and out of the prison of self-interest in order to experience the freedom of shared opportunity.

As greater numbers of people experience the increased dissolution of the personal will and the lure of selfish pursuits, the level of collective goodwill and philanthropy elevates.

The idea of global goodwill can be regarded as an organic movement for planetary peace. Eventually, it will infiltrate the hearts and minds of groups, religious institutions, corporations and societal systems resulting in the most authentic transformation of global consciousness we have yet to witness.

The universal energy of goodwill may be the healing salve that completely reverses the ailing relationships between the majority of human beings and their collective nations.

This consummate force of the divine intelligence flowing through the illumined minds of people everywhere victoriously shatters and consumes all barriers of separation and hatred, revealing the radiant truth lying behind all creation, that of love and unity.

It is this universal realization that stimulates the remembrance of the will to do good, the will to do unto others as you would have done to you; the golden rule for a truly peaceful civilization.

When the majority of people on Earth are being rapidly oriented towards good, it seems certain that the false reality of suffering will disappear completely. Terrorism, violence, disease, poverty, famine, war and the plethora of separation-inspired creations will dissolve in the face of goodwill and global cooperation.

This is even contagious at the micro level. In planting the seed of goodwill in your neighbor's garden, you bear witness to the joy that blooms as a result in the hearts of those around you.

Multiply that single seed by the millions of people currently gracing the Earth with their combined efforts, and we have a veritable garden of goodwill continuing to spring up all across the globe.

The sheer demonstration of our numerical strength is a testament to the profound influence we can have on the mass collective consciousness through our inward alignment to Divine Will.

As a result of this inner calibration, we are continuing to plant the magnetic seed of the future in the new energetic grids of consciousness. This will insure that all people can reap and share in the abundant harvest of love and the spirit of global interdependence.

One person sincerely practicing goodwill in a circle of family and friends can completely change attitudes. Goodwill practiced among groups in any nation, by political and religious parties in any nation and among nations can revolutionize the world.

Let's join together to sow the seeds of goodwill in ourselves and across the globe in an effort to furnish the Earth with paradise gardens of universal peace, grown and nurtured in the hearts of all humanity.

INVOCATION TO THE WILL
OF DIVINE PRESENCE

Dear Masterful Presence and Divine Self,

I am completely dedicated to your divine plan and hereby surrender the personal will. Make visible in my hands and use the fullness of your willful power.

I no longer claim any power as my own, for I now claim you, the only and all-conquering Presence in my home, my life, my work and my experiences. I acknowledge your all-knowing wisdom and command of all things.

As my consciousness is fixed upon an achievement, your invincible Presence and intelligence takes control and brings the appropriate response into my experience quickly, even with the speed of my aligned thought.

Great Divine Presence, I know that you are the ruler over time, place and space; therefore, you require only the eternal now to bring your every perfection into visible activity.

I stand absolutely firm in the full acceptance of this, now and forever, and I shall not allow my mind to waver from it, for at last, I know we are one.

Divine Presence, almighty I AM.

"It is through my increasing capacity as a thinker that enables me to enter into the superconscious mind housed within my own individual being. All is truly within."

SHIFTING POLARIZATION
TO DIVINE MIND

I t is the natural course of initiation that progresses us towards an eventual fusion of the human personality with that of the soul.

This process of synthesis is symbolically described as an elevation of consciousness into the higher mental field, or, into the polarization of divine mind. As a step-by-step consciousness shift, we eventually reform ourselves into a brand new human design that can house higher light intelligence.

This all begins with changing how we think and discarding the way we've been trained to think. This requires us to step outside of the box and outside of the walls of rigid programming. To do this, we must learn how to perceive much differently.

It may sound simple; yet, changing our thought structure is one of the most challenging of all because our inherited conditioning runs ultra-deep, often hidden away in the many layers of the subconscious.

A major block that prevents our expansion into the greater self is the polarized perception that perceives from the emotions. This especially pertains to the highly charged emotional patterns that are used to respond to life experiences.

This covers the gamut of human emotion including the cause and effect of our fears and doubts plus attaching hold to our self-identity and its desires.

These types of emotionally based programs cause core internal conflict and keep us blinded to any other possible reality. We really get into trouble when we settle into polarized perspectives that are always tipping to the side of the emotional filter. Charging emotions are often what direct our affairs and even color our personalities, so much, that this is how we are self-identified.

In humanity's current evolutionary leap, the code of the highly polarized emotional body changes. It eventually neutralizes, which triggers an immense vibrational upgrade. We become repolarized and recalibrated to the mental body.

To understand this term, mental body, is to know that our mind actually expresses in more than one way. We have a lower concrete mind and a higher spiritual, or abstract mind. These two aspects of the mind enable us to exist and communicate in both the physical dimension and in spiritual realities.

This is our inherent encoding. You could say that we are naturally divine. We are spirits having a human experience versus humans having a spiritual experience.

The idea of emotional body upgrade and to be polarized in the mental body means to vibrate in synthesis with the spiritual mind, an aspect of who we are as light intelligence.

Djwal Kul was a very wise Tibetan master who taught in the tradition of ancient esoteric spirituality. He brought forth much understanding about the science of spiritual initiation including this subject matter of the great repolarization.

To paraphrase, he once conveyed that the human race is progressing into an era whereby it will function as minds; when intelligence will be stronger than desire, and when thought powers will be used for appeal and guidance of the world, a world where now physical and emotional means are employed. He said love is the great unifier but the mind is the main creative factor and the utilizer of the energies of the cosmos.

His teachings share that the spiritual aspirant, together with an integrated personality, can gradually bring the emotional body under the control of mental energy. Then, the individual's physical activity is not so much implemented by instinct or desire, but through thought energy, which is dedicated to and expresses the nature of humanity's evolutionary plan.

This is exactly where we are evolving. When we are mentally polarized, our consciousness is focused in the intelligence of the abstract mind. This level of consciousness is like a doorway, which provides access to a blended union with our higher mind, or Divine Presence, our greater aspect that truly runs the show.

In this transition, our human mind becomes a receiving station and channel through which our Divine Presence expresses.

From this place of mental polarization, the emotional desires of the personality are transcended into the purposeful aspirations of the soul. We find ourselves transitioning away from an "emotionally responding human" to one that feels deeply and just knows. This is because the emotional body is finally stable and integrated as a holistic vessel.

Moreover, being polarized in the mental body means that our higher abilities organically come online such as intuition, telepathy, and multidimensional perception. These are skillsets that cannot be grasped emotionally but mentally as the bridge to the higher mind is built.

Upgrading into mental body polarization is a primary phase of spiritual initiation and one that is not achieved overnight, by any means. Emotional body stabilization is known to be one of the longest phases of human soul initiation.

It is a phased process that requires utmost dedication and practice to calm the triggers and release the many attachments of the human senses. It also requires us to renovate and retrain our systems of belief.

Let's dive deeper into some ideas surrounding this retraining of the mechanism of thought.

THE PRINCIPLE OF THOUGHT MANIFESTATION

It was been previously shared that the one single characteristic of this new consciousness that drastically differs from the current human matrix is that it lives in accordance with divine principle. These are the immutable laws of nature that are the foundation stones upon which humanity's new framework of consciousness is built.

The universal laws of nature serve as great spiritual truths. They are the governing forces that determine every aspect of creation. When you abide by them, you co-create circumstances under these laws. As a creator in a physical reality, the rules are quite simple. What you believe is true, is what you are going to experience.

Studies in quantum physics have confirmed that thoughts create our realities. Scientists have discovered the mirror of their own minds inside the atom, where the existence and the behavior of the particles depend on the intent of the scientist.

Regarding intent and thought manifestation, there is a universal law called, mentalism, which embodies the idea that the entire universe is an infinite living mind, a consciousness of which everything and everyone is an integral aspect.

Mentalism is saying that all creation exists in the mind of the one Absolute Source, and likewise, through this reflection, our personal lives really exist in our own minds. Quite simply, this is saying that perception is what creates reality.

This supreme, infinite mind intelligence is a revealing mirror to reflect how humans, who are made in its "image and likeness", can create mentally in the microcosm just as Prime Creator creates the ever-expanding macrocosm.

As an extension of this brilliance, consider that your personal reality is fabricated from the perceptions you hold. Seven billion humans share the same planet Earth, yet frequently embracing very different perspectives. We are all projecting parts of the same holographic illusion who operate from the screen of our fragmented minds to create a physical reality experience. This is quite profound.

We each construct our own universes with our creative minds, which are an expression of the one prime creator force. Therefore, it is through our increasing capacity as "thinkers" that enables us to enter into the superconscious mind housed within our own individual being. All *is* truly within.

To do this is to declare and authentically live our eternal unity with the superconscious mind of our creator, as the individualized Divine Presence. The physical body and everything else in our life come into alignment as soon as we self-realize and embody this fundamental unity.

From this state of resonance, we open into the innate understanding that we already have all that we need within our own powerful being. It has only been through our own separated imaginings that we have experienced reflections of suffering and limitation in our lives.

It may simply be a matter of transitioning our thinking to engage a more dominant thought structure as one with divine mind in order to reach our highest potential to where thought can aspire.

You may have heard the expression that we are "Gods on training wheels." This could not be truer!

You are a creator made in the image and likeness of your prime creator parent. Therefore, all realities lie within you and all realities are created by you. Physical reality is created by what you deem it to be.

There is no outside. Nothing comes from the outside.

*"I am transitioning my thinking to engage
a more dominant thought structure, as one with
Divine Mind, in order to reach my highest potential
to where thought can aspire."*

TRANSITIONING INTO A NEW THOUGHT STRUCTURE

To attain true self-liberation, we are required to let go of attaching emotional desire and over-identification to the physical form while illuminating more of the mind's functions.

It is not an easy task to transcend desire and our emotional holds to the material world. It has been said that this phase of transition is one of the most challenging of all. It requires strength of will, steadfast determination and a constant reorientation of the mind so that the personality self can be held sure and steady in the light of the soul.

The doors have finally opened to us, as a collective, to enter into the greater mental fields, which provide clear and pure access to supreme knowledge. This avails us the real potential for complete soul union and the resultant embodiment of Divine Presence in outer world expression.

This chapter shares many ideas on how you can neutralize your emotional body field and repolarize to the mental body, as a seamless synthesis with your higher mind.

There are many effective practices and disciplines for making this monumental shift while dispelling the hindering false formations of consciousness. Following are some examples of how to think in a brand new way and how to manifest in accordance with divine principle.

PERCEIVE AS ABSOLUTE CONSCIOUSNESS

It is important to gain understanding of who and what you are as a vast multidimensional consciousness field. This is because a very, very minute fragment of your consciousness is incarnated as a human form.

Even if this is not so clear for you, form a habit to look at your life from a bird's eye view; especially if you feel confused or stuck in some emotions.

The habit of always regarding the bigger picture can be developed and practiced so that the consciousness remains attuned at all times to the truer nature of your being.

You are expanding your self to rise above the human condition. This is to learn, first and foremost, how to live truly as an observer and then to simply be the witness to the emotions that are rising and falling.

While you are a witness to your life, remember that there is only one consciousness at play. You are made in its image and likeness.

This omnipresence weaves your life and everyone else's as well. It does not take sides because it exists in everything. It is the active intelligence in all things that we see, breathe, feel, think, touch and consume.

Keep coming back to the realization that you are one with it all; not separated. When we are in neutralized awareness, we do not attach to our struggles, rather, we see them as a learning ground for consciousness advancement.

Everything is here for a reason. The circumstances in your life are giving a perfect experience for the soul and its evolutionary advancement.

Always return to the realization that you are an extension of creation.

OPEN INTO NEW THOUGHT

To neutralize emotional polarity, it is necessary to open into a brand new way of thinking and perceiving. This requires some training to bridge the human intellect with divine knowing.

No matter how smart we are at the human level, we simply cannot advance our consciousness through the mind's intellect alone. It occurs through the influence of our Divine Presence, the higher mental body that enters into us as pure knowing.

The more that you let go of what you think you know, the more the light absorbs you and your higher vibratory self over-rides the human energy system with upgraded channels and circuitry.

This allows higher messaging to be received and properly translated, altogether bypassing the use of the emotional faculty. Through much sensitization of your energy field, you can develop as a channel for the Divine Presence to express more fully and more purely.

This is an initiation of mental body repolarization and sets into greater momentum the building of a new thought structure. This involves remembering and then anchoring into the physical reality what you already know in the expanded versions of the self.

You are light intelligence. Your brain is built upon God cells. You are naturally endowed with brilliance. There is a divine intelligence and directing influence that pervades every cell of your human form.

Your cells want to remember this and to be released from the binding thought forms that clothe them in limitation. It may simply be a matter of transitioning your thinking to engage a more dominant thought structure, as one with Divine Mind, in order to reach your highest potential to where 'thought' can aspire.

The animal kindred has never lost its instinct for the very reason that it is incapable of building an adverse thought structure.

For example, when a bird migrates to a certain destination, sometimes traveling for thousands of miles, it never loses the direction. It is not thinking about whether or not it can accomplish the task. The guiding instrument is right within its tiny brain cells.

Humans are far more capable than animals or birds; yet, we have allowed ourselves to adapt to a very foreign and distorted way of thinking. Throughout human history, we have been hypnotized into believing in negative conditions and their outer appearances.

The bottom line is that you are dynamically coded as brilliant and you can be restored to this original perfection. Yet, only through a new system of thought can this happen.

You have never lost the capacity to have supreme intelligence. It was just over-ridden by another system, a 'free will' system of thought. Prime Creator gifted us the abilities to have free rein in this human reality. This is why so many of us choose to surrender the free will because it only gets us in sticky, icky trouble!

Physical reality is a series of projections and reflections. Whatever you believe or regard as true for you, this truth manifests, whether it is negative or positive, limiting or limitless.

This is why it is often said, "think big", or, "believe in yourself and all things are possible." The universe responds to each and every thought we have.

Stressful conditions have absolutely no power over us, except that which we give to them. The moment we cease feeding the condition with our charging energy, it no longer has life and, thus, it ceases to exist altogether.

In our refusal to accept limitation or any form of negativity in our life, we make a grand departure from the paradigm of suffering.

From this moment forward, you can choose to simply stop all thinking from this old thought system that perceives limitation of any type.

Absolutely refuse any and all appearances of limitation in your life. Refuse to perceive it as limitation. This is the difference. Refuse to perceive it as limitation. Then, you will no longer abide within it.

You have all that you need within your own inner powerful self as one with your Divine Presence, the higher mind.

All you have to do is simply shift the way that you think. Striving, struggle, hard work, suffering; these all come from the old system of thought and from believing in limitation, from perceiving that you are limited.

YOU ARE ALWAYS SUPPORTED

There is a divine principle that expresses, "You are always taken care of and provided for." This is stated so simply, yet interestingly, is one of the most challenging truths to embrace.

Your Divine Presence is the God power. It governs all manifestation in your life perfectly. It is the power producing it and the force sustaining it.

Have complete reliance upon that which moves in the deepest side of your nature and what is referred to as, the God within.

When you stand unified with this divine principle, all is magnetized to you in spontaneous flow, in perfect timing, and in just the right quantity. No strenuous effort is required. No affirmations are needed. Even the idea of prayer becomes obsolete. "Want" and "need" become signals to what is already in manifesting motion.

The truth is, everything is always here and always present. The moment you recognize a need, it is already being fulfilled. It is absolutely impossible to need anything if it were not already in existence.

This is indicated by the very fact that "need" has shown up and is expressing. You confidently accept the fact implied in the need that the solution is already coming towards you. If it were not already in momentum, the thought would not even enter into your awareness.

To embody this principle is to vibrationally align with this new way to perceive and carry out your tasks. You do not have to go out there so aggressively and get it. You do not have to force something to happen.

Material reality is purely a vibration of energy. Therefore, align yourself, first, to the vibration of the need itself. This goes back to the Law of Action. Act as if the need is already fulfilling.

As soon as you observe a need arising, change your frequency channel to the program you want to see. Do this by knowing, with great certainty, that this need is the beacon alerting you that it is already being fulfilled according to your highest good.

The moment that you come into vibrational alignment by unifying with the completed condition, it begins to express outwardly. In this, the energy of need becomes a magnetic tool.

This is the new energy. We are living life through divine principle and this can be applied to everything in our reality.

It may be easy to understand this from a mental perspective. The real challenge, however, is to apply it to daily life. How do we genuinely open into a new thought structure? How do we shift the perception and make sure it sticks?

Always remember, perception creates reality. Your world manifests according to how you choose to interpret it! You can choose to live in a world that is perceived as full of division, hate, and separation. Alternatively, you can also choose to live in a world that is perceived as loving, peaceful, and abundant.

If you are experiencing limitation in this moment, remove your attention off of the appearance and place it, instead, upon your Divine Presence; the only giver of support that there is.

It is from this state of knowing, that every question is answered and every thought that you think produces a vibration that coheres your energy. If you stand firm and determined in this, your reality is guaranteed to reflect a considerably different picture.

Remember, you are made of divine essence. You are one with divine mind. You live inside the very body of absolute source. You are divinity through the form.

Command that you see only truth and only the truth can manifest. See only what you want to manifest. Refuse to see anything else.

When you recognize perfection, you are that perfection. There is no other recognition. It is all God. You, as an extension of that divinity, are the creator of your reality.

"Reality reflects my state of mind.
State of mind is the fuel to manifestation.
As I perceive, life expresses."

THRIVING THROUGH THE
REFLECTIVE MIRROR

The laws of metaphysics give great clues to the way that physical reality works in the schoolroom called Earth. This next statement really sums it up.

You are a creator God in training.

This training is all about mastering the self. You can look at your life as if immersed in a game. The game token, to help you skillfully maneuver through the matrix of projection, is your apparatus of thought. Each frequency of your thought is coded to materialize in the visible realm.

In other words, your thoughts birth live energetic substance into motion. This stream of living light energy then responds back to you through a superimposed projection upon a reflective screen that appears right in front of you.

You, as the thinking game master, are then living out an experience from what is showing up on your personal life screen. Everything you experience is a reality molded out of your thoughts and emotions. Whatever you predominantly think about is creating the hologram of your existence, and that which you may think is solid and outside of you.

What you perceive are the sensory-based projections from your own mind. These mental perceptions attract circumstances, situations and people to play in the role as your game pieces.

The reality that you perceive around you is actually created *from* you, whether consciously or unconsciously. Your thoughts control every single thing that happens in your own unique and individual reality.

To make sense of this, let's go back to microcosmic and macrocosmic principles. As the saying goes, "as above so below, as within so without." You are the part and you are the whole. You are both one and the same, and are right now experiencing the whole as a part, all in a world of matter. This physicalized reality is contained within the totality of your consciousness.

As an aspect of the whole, what is true for you is true for God, the supreme awareness that pervades all life. You, as one with God, are the thought and you, as one with God, are the thinker. You are the creator. As a creator in a physical reality, the rules are quite simple. What you believe is what you are going to experience.

Everything in your physical reality is made up from projections of consciousness.

All realities lie within you and all realities are created by you. Physical reality is created by what you deem it to be. There is no outside. Nothing comes from the outside. You are your own entire universe.

What this means is that reality reflects your state of mind. Life is created from your beliefs and the physical you is the sum total of all of your thoughts and feelings. Everything in your life is reflecting your thought vibration.

Whatever you are thinking, feeling and projecting, whether consciously or unconsciously, goes right into the mirror of physical reality. This mirror responds by giving you back a reflection. These reflections form your life experiences.

To make positive use of this information, take some time to sincerely look at yourself and observe how your entire life has been created according to what you believe to be true. Then, contemplate all of the times that you have changed your beliefs and, as a result, new outer reflections appeared.

This is evident in all sorts of personal events including your relationships, jobs, and projects. You have only been limited by how you have believed. Life is a direct product of your definitions about it! By changing these definitions, you change the reality in which you exist. It is as simple as that.

You are in control of life's mirror by what you perceive to be true or what you believe you deserve. As a powerful creator, to change any pictures in your manifesting reality, simply shift the thought that holds the belief in place. You have to first make this change on the inside so that mirror of outer experience can reflect a different picture.

For instance, let's say that a travel opportunity comes your way and you really want to go. The financial means, however, do not currently appear in your bank account. If you say that you cannot go because you cannot afford it, then the doors to that potential experience will most likely remain closed. There is a belief system that equates the appearance of money with the means to opportunity.

If you constantly affirm your desire, however, and hold unwavering commitment to the manifestation, the trip has a much better chance of happening. You are setting the creation wheels into motion through your affirmative thought. The reflections bouncing back will mirror your determination towards the manifestation.

It's amazing what can happen and in ways previously unimagined. You probably have experienced this type of scenario.

The truth is, you do not need to work so hard or force issues to make change happen. The idea of "trying" to accomplish is not really necessary. It is to just be the observer, in coherence with your life's reflections. Then, through these reflections, you can make adjustments in your consciousness along the way.

RELATIONSHIPS GIVE A REFLECTIVE MESSAGE

Let's apply these ideas to our most intimate relationships. All of the closest relationships currently appearing in your life are mirroring your beliefs, including the thoughts you have about yourself.

Some of these relationship aspects may be kind, happy and loving. Others might be experiencing pain and struggle. Some of these people in your intimate sphere might be reflecting your deep subconscious programming.

There are also those individuals that come into our life and seem to completely invalidate what we stand for. This level of reflection can have many meanings and does not always mean that this is about your invalidation. It might be an invitation for you to stand strong in your personal truth.

You might be mirroring back to this person an image of someone who maintains an empowered and sovereign posture. This could also give back to each of you the importance of compromise or to see another perspective and allowing another version of truth to co-exist with yours, without going into judgment.

All truths are true in the ultimate sense because we are all creating our own reality. No one's truth is any more or less valid than any other.

The bottom line is that any bonded relationship is reflecting an important message back to the self. Every situation has the potential for you to learn and expand. When you are as clear as you can be about the definitions you give to life, you can observe your relationships and determine whether or not they match up to the definitions you prefer to have.

The first and most important step to create the reality you prefer is to make sure you are always validating the self. Invalidating yourself brings invalidating experiences and often lots of drama and conflict in your relating.

People come and go. The revolving door of relationships reflects your evolution as a thinking intelligence and sentient being. As your perceptions change, it is inevitable that your relationships will change too. Some will remain and change with you. Some will go away completely.

This is natural due to the constantly changing mirror of perception. Each person is relevant and plays a part in your phases of mastering the self.

Knowing this, there is no reason, whatsoever, to blame or negatively judge any person or life situation. You are creating it all!

Whatever it is that you perceive about another individual, you are forcing that quality into your own experience, whether negative or positive. The moment you think about either perfection or imperfection, you bring that quality into your own mirror of experience.

This is why the only desirable feeling to be projected out is love, pure unselfish love that holds you and everyone else in his or her highest potential. Each person is really a part of you, which is essentially your self-created reflection in the mirror.

To understand any relationship more clearly, first get in touch with your own belief that has created the person to be in front of you to mirror their reflection back to you.

If another, more preferred reality is desired with another, shift your beliefs that hold the vibration of your relationship in place.

Come up with a different way of relating that mirrors the frequency of your preferred reality.

If you desire to attract a certain person into your reality screen, adjust your vibration to match that particular frequency.

For example, you have probably heard testimony from people who attracted a new life partner into their lives after writing down and constantly affirming all of the qualities in the type of person that was being sought.

This is an example of emanating the very vibration of what you want to manifest. By matching your vibration with the object of desire, you enter into an experience that corresponds to the very vibration of your thought and feeling.

Above all, keep validating the self. Allow yourself to see in all others an aspect of your own beautiful being. We are all interconnected; we are all the individual parts that form an integral whole.

To be in the highest relationship with life, you love the self by loving all others. You love all others by loving the self. This love of self will automatically attract many lovers into your life.

In summary, always remember this truth...

Reality reflects your state of mind.

State of mind is the fuel to manifestation.

As you perceive, life expresses.

This is why the concept of thinking about what you want is so powerful. Thoughts literally create every single experience and circumstance in your life. You are truly a creator God in training, disciplining your body to serve as channel to receive the currents of universal mind.

Once you understand these principles and master the 'thinking', your new creations take on majestic form because you know how reality works in a dense matter existence.

This is why the idea of embodying the Divine Presence as your greatest expression and human potential is not such a far-fetched idea. You are right on track!

Have fun with this and see how far you can go with the highest thoughts that you can imagine.

"I place high value upon my life and how I am choosing to navigate it in order to learn and evolve. I honor my choices and am consistently living the true frequency of my core values."

SELF-VALIDATION IS A
MASTERFUL REFLECTION

Thoughts are powerful things, especially when we consistently validate the privilege of life that we have been gifted.

Self-validation is accepting yourself, your thoughts and feelings as real and true for you. This means to consistently validate all of your experiences and situations as a blessing, full of meaning and an orchestration for your highest good.

It can be no other way. You are within God and God is within you. God, as your individualized Divine Presence, is experiencing itself through you as a human channel. This is your highest alignment and truth.

One of the greatest obstacles to moving deeper into union with our Divine Presence is self-invalidation. Most people have some form of this running in the background of their consciousness.

Invalidation results from the consciousness programming that tenaciously holds on to the negative perceptions we have about the self.

The mind's ability to generate invalidating thoughts is very powerful when it is working off of old programming. It is easy to fall into the habit of invalidating the self, especially when we have been wounded from past conditioning and trauma. Most of the time it is done unconsciously.

Yet, the mirror of life is certainly busy, constantly reflecting our invalidating thoughts. These stem from self-judgment and all the ways that we devalue our expression, which only causes a personal platform of pain and insecurity.

For example, if you constantly say that you do not like something and still remain engaged, this invalidates your truer desire. We often feel this discontent in many areas such as our jobs, projects, financial scenarios and relationships.

How many times do we say that we are frustrated, tired of this or that or not happy, yet, do nothing about it? These statements completely invalidate the fields of blessing energy that are always embracing us.

If you are feeling tired or complete with something, then bring change to the situation so that there is an opening for the energy to shift. Being tired or frustrated is a signal to act and to do something different, or, to shift the perception about the situation so that the resulting reflection changes.

Much of this resistance and judgment about the self also stems from really old habitual thought. These embedded patterns must be rewritten so that more wholesome thought processes can become the new feedback pathway.

With more wholesome thought patterns in place, it is far easier to let go of resistance, tune in to our inner resources and move forward with empowered self-confidence.

Be vigilant about keeping a watchful eye to ensure that you are constantly validating yourself in all that you say, think and do.

THE MIRROR OF JUDGMENT

Negative judgment projected towards another person is another area in which we self-invalidate.

How easy is it to judge others who choose a different path than us? No matter what the situation is, when we negatively judge, attack or condemn another person's choices, we are only invalidating and harming the self.

How could we ever completely know the life plan of another soul? How could we ever truly know how that soul's Divine Presence is guiding their life stream?

In projections of judgment, we are attaching to the very vibration that we claim is not our own. Life is a mirror and in many instances, when we judge, we are judging an aspect or pattern still contained within our self.

Through judgment, we are placing attaching identification with the condition being judged and therefore, opening ourselves up to creating that same vibration within ourselves.

Recognize what is true for you and allow other people to have full equality for their choices. Do your best to be a neutral observer towards others while remaining clear and true to your own choices and preferred resonance. This is the difference between judgment and preference.

Here is another scenario. Have you ever come across someone or something directly on your path and just want to turn a blind's eye to it or push it away? If you attempt to get rid of anything in your life, you will quickly find that there is nowhere for this energy to be stuffed. There is no outside. You are the complete universe of your experience.

Attempting to push something away that you do not prefer is invalidating your immediate present reality.

The harder you try to push it away, the more energy you actually give it to spring back, because it has nowhere to go. It could very well generate what appears to be the repetitive cycle of highly polarized negativity.

The solution to this resistance is always about acceptance and allowance. If something discomforting is arising, regardless of why, it is presenting itself for a reason. It is like a beacon, alerting your attention. It is likely giving a reflective message about something to reconcile within yourself.

THE HABIT OF SELF-DOUBT

Another looping habit, which often goes unnoticed, comes from the memory imprint of doubt. Doubt stems from such beliefs that you are not worthy, that you are not good enough, not capable enough or feeling you are not supported.

Self-doubt is one of the biggest sabotaging energies that brings instant disconnect from the clear and radiant flows of Divine Presence.

Doubt lives in the memory field and it stems from the habit of constantly invalidating the self and who you are as an empowered, sovereign creator. This one too, goes unnoticed when we are doing it.

An example of invalidating the self through doubt is when we buy into belief systems that are not necessarily in congruence with our truer feelings or what we really prefer to believe. Do you ever change your preferred choices in life in order to accommodate someone else's opinion or their idea of what you should be doing?

Begin recognizing any areas of your life that you are self-invalidating through doubt. Above all, stand strong for how and what you choose to believe and express. It is just as valid as any other way.

If you invalidate your deeply felt preferences and inspiration, then you are invalidating the blessing that is constantly being showered upon you. You cease the invalidation by following your preferences and creating your reality based upon those preferences.

If you do not live your preferences, this is not honoring the self. This is not honoring your Divine Presence because you are discounting its impulses. Instead, it opens you up to attract people, situations and experiences into your life that reflect and validate this dishonoring.

Be super clear on your intentions for divine embodiment. Keep moving towards your desired preferences by constantly and unwaveringly acting upon your highest feelings of inspiration. This is really all you have to do.

Inspiration comes from your Divine Presence. The manifesting doors will open so fast in response to you simply acting upon these feelings. Just walk through that door of inspired thought, without any hesitation.

When you act upon this inner feeling state, you actually ground and center in the now moment, a highly alchemical field from where all creation springs forth. This instantly opens the door for more information to be revealed.

You can master the game of life simply by acting only upon whatever it is that you prefer and what gives you inner jubilation.

Even if you are experiencing some struggle or confusion as to what you really want, at the very least, clearly define what your preferences are in life, down to the simplest of things. Then, step-by-step, begin to match these preferences by acting them out.

Prime the pump by just starting to live your preferred resonance. A new day will dawn. Stress releases. Internal pressure goes away.

The light naturally comes in because you are living your personal truth.

The reality you choose to create and experience is determined by your attitude. This sets up the sequence of causes and effects in your life. Every option is always available to you.

You do not have to make something happen. You allow a certain flow to come into your life by being tuned into the preferred resonance that represents that flow. Just like a radio, you get the channel that you are dialed into!

Recognize that whatever inspires you the most is the gateway to the most efficient and effortless way that you can coalesce your energy. Inspiration is what tells you that this direction, situation or thing is the most 'you'.

Whatever is mirroring to you this level of elevated feeling, know that this is your authentic self. This is what you are all about.

Self-validation is the master's reflection.

*"My presence and very existence is
founded upon the surrender to my one
and true Beloved."*

EXEMPLIFYING THE PILLARS
OF DIVINE EMBODIMENT

I n our development as an enlightened collective, great emphasis is placed upon embodiment, as in divine embodiment. "To embody" the divine means to personify, exemplify and give tangible form to our great spiritual presence.

What does it take to shift into this greater potential as a real life, grounded expression?

It is certainly different for everyone. Maintaining clear vision of your evolving potential is an important step. If you are well on the path of self-realization, you probably know by now there is no real shortcut. There is no magic pill that one can take to make it instantaneous.

To embody means to merge back, consciously, with the source of your existence. What does this really mean, practically speaking?

Following are some real and tangible occurrences experienced by many spiritual aspirants.

For one, it is like your antennas are constantly attuned to higher messaging. The human mind is under the influence of much more powerful force. There is a sense of an overriding, greater will energy that is always present and gently nudging.

Overall sensitivity to energy increases and the heart feels deeply, no matter what it is. There is a constant yearning for one's greatest beloved, which is a feeling that goes far beyond human emotion.

Realizing the Divine Self has proven, time and time again, to be a well-trodden path of purification. It is a passionate and highly personal endeavor requiring unwavering dedication, perseverance, constant surrender and a great deal of patience. This is indeed the work of an entire lifetime.

No matter how far along we may think we are, there is always another door of humility to open. Until we get it right, there seems to be one experience after another to remind us of the vulnerable human nature. Therefore, constant purification ensues to prepare the body to house its greater light.

Why is it so difficult for us to accept who we really are? This idea may sound super simple yet in today's hyper glamourized world, there is a great deal of pressure to be something we are not. It is so darn easy to be swayed off track, especially when there is no true foundation to ground our transformation.

The process of embodying our divine nature is like building a house. Its strength and stability lie in the foundation. This house, however, is more like a mansion, requiring a much bigger and stronger platform.

So often, spiritual aspirants want the final result without assuring that the necessary grounding is in place. There is a tendency to disregard crucial steps along the way. Yet, no matter what anyone tells you, there is no instant program, teaching or miraculous cosmic event that can bring anyone into this high state of alchemy.

It takes time, deep inner work and whole lot of patience. It also requires a very strong and very stable foundation. This foundation must be securely in place to elevate the vibration into one's greater expression.

There are four primary pillars to this foundation building that give the needed support and reinforcement. These grounding rods are absolutely interdependent and mutually supportive.

If you were to ever come across an individual who has these four attributes fully anchored and integrated, you will find someone who is authentically embodied and who operates from Divine Presence.

FOUNDATIONAL PILLAR #1: SELF-VALIDATION

The very first pillar to grounding your foundation of divine embodiment is self-validation. This is fully accepting and loving your self, just as you are right now together with all of your experiences.

We have already touched upon this pivotal subject matter in a previous chapter, however, it bears repeating.

You validate the self by placing high value upon your life and how you are choosing to navigate it in order to learn and evolve. You honor your choices and are consistently living the true frequency of your core values.

This means to consistently validate all of your experiences and situations as a blessing, full of meaning and an orchestration for your highest good. It can be no other way. You are within God, and God is within you. God is experiencing itself through you as a human channel. This is your highest alignment and truth.

It is easy to fall into the habit of invalidating the self. Most of the time it is done unconsciously. Yet, the mirror of life is certainly busy, constantly reflecting experiences of invalidation.

Remember, everything in your current reality is mirroring those thoughts you hold or previously projected about the self.

When you are misaligned to your true core self, you may feel this reflection as rising fear, anxiety or as lacking something. You might feel a sense of despair and like you are living on a giant wheel of pain and discomfort.

Look at any definitions and beliefs that you hold that de-value your self in any way. Most of the time, these are habitual thoughts that are unconscious and on autopilot. Become extra vigilant to how you regard the self.

Shift away from any negative thinking by learning how to place yourself as the priority. This is not in a selfish way but to make sure your needs are adequately being met. Make sure that you are not devaluing or downplaying your self worth.

To have a high level of self-worth means never allowing yourself to be defined by outside forces, including other people's opinions. You are accepting yourself wholeheartedly at all times despite your flaws, weaknesses, and limitations. It's about recognizing the real value of who you are in this present moment.

Only when you place high value upon yourself as being worthy, supported and loved, holding yourself in the same value that your Creator holds you, only then will your heart truly radiate. This builds your attractor field to draw in experiences that mirror that love of self. This includes relationships, abundance and creative opportunities.

Another remarkable way that we bring validation into our lives is when we act upon our inspiration. You will know that you are aligned and living your true fundamental self when you are inspired and act upon your inspiration without hesitation. You live according to your preferences and experience these inspired flows as joy, creativity and love.

To be inspired means that your mind has reached a stage where you are consciously and positively under the direction of your Divine Presence. This vibrational resonance is your true, core, natural being.

The quality of self-validation is so important because your next steps and greater openings will only be as effective as the energy you give to it all. The real motivating power comes through you!

FOUNDATIONAL PILLAR #2: DIVINE INTIMACY

An important foundational pillar to support the embodied radiance of your greater self is divine intimacy.

So often, spiritual aspirants yearn for deeper connection with the greater self. They want to know the life purpose and soul plan. There is a longing to feel and acknowledge the greater self-expression in a much more tangible and noticeable way so that one can truly thrive from this resonance.

To be in divine intimacy is one of the highest attainable states possible for the human experience. Your presence and very existence is founded upon the surrender and adoration to your one and true Beloved.

This is speaking into a union of love with your Creator. The nature of this force of love is to expand, and to such a degree that it naturally spills over to have an immense influence on a multitude of souls.

To arrive into this level of deep intimacy with the God within, one must first have intimacy with the self. This refers to truly loving the self, fully and completely. Are you capable of having deep intimacy with yourself?

When we know and experience ourselves as one with our core self, really loving and attending to the self, this becomes the pure mirror of our thought energy. Self-validation, self-respect and self-acknowledgement put us right in touch with the Divine Presence of our being.

Self-love is the gateway to divine intimacy. To love yourself at the deepest level is to simultaneously know and experience the Divine Presence manifesting in your life.

God, expressing as the Divine Presence within you, is the authority of the entire universe. The Divine Presence hears, sees, thinks, feels and responds to only perfection on its level of cosmic service.

As you consistently give adoration, feel gratitude and qualify your every activity through this energy stream, your daily positive impact upon life is immeasurable.

Maintaining an intimate relationship with your source of life is like being constantly with your dearest beloved and most trusted friend. Many people, even those who claim to be spiritually awake, are without this endearment.

To be consciously disconnected from our creator, we are simply not operating from the wholeness of life. This is the main reason why we may feel limited and with a sense of emptiness, even though our lives may seem to be very full.

To truly embody the Divine Presence, we cannot go through life being busy and with a long list of to-dos without often stopping to assure deep and intimate communion with our source.

This is referring to a deepening in your feeling body to really experience yourself as one with this eternal identity. It is like you have a best friend who is always there encouraging you into your greater potential.

This intimacy can be felt as an unwavering sense of trust and knowing. Doubts vanish as soon as you create a rhythm of openly sharing with the greater you.

One of the biggest challenges is that ideas of divinity can be intellectualized versus having a direct and authentic experience. Our human intelligence is often asserted to understand the spiritual side of life. There can also be adherence to dogma and its many speculations of truth about what it means to be self-realized.

We also must be extra cautious about aligning with those who adamantly proclaim a specific system or method as the only way to attain enlightenment.

We can only go so far with the ambiguous mind; only to discover that the door remains closed into more expanded dimensions. It is because we often do not give ourselves quality time to have the direct experience of the Divine Presence, or to deeply contemplate this influence in our lives.

While spiritual philosophies, tools and outside resources are helpful to advance our intellectual understandings; they are not able to provide us with a tangible experience of the chief energy that is truly taking care of us. In fact, we run the risk of becoming overly dependent on external information in lieu of a deep and intimate relationship with the one true source of it all.

The Divine Presence will never be revealed through the human intellect. To try and do so will only leave us defending personal beliefs based upon the theories and ideas of others. A very big challenge for many people is to surrender; surrender to the higher mind so that this greater influence can be the one and only navigator.

It is of extraordinary importance to develop a deeper level of intimacy with your greater self. Without it, there is only the intellectual response from the human mind that is ruled by the ego and its tactile senses.

From time to time we have glimpses of this great Divine Presence revealing itself in our life; receiving exactly what we needed at exactly the right time with little to no effort, seeming as though by a miracle. Our joy now is to fully realize this supremely positive influence is available to us in each and every moment.

It is when we are at one and in coherence with the greater self in daily communion that we are led down the path of non-stop opening doors.

Acknowledge this part of you! Talk to this Presence, love this Presence, know that the greater self is revealing itself to you all of the time. These reflections of intimate communion are always there.

FOUNDATIONAL PILLAR #3: INTEGRITY

The third foundational pillar to divine embodiment is integrity.

This is the state of being whole and undivided. It is the quality of being honest and having strong moral principles. Other descriptive words that go with this foundational alignment are sincere, virtuous, honorable, truthful and trustworthiness.

It goes even deeper.

To be divinely embodied, you are holistically integrated from within. This brings pristine and seamless integrity to your entire energy field.

» Integrity exists in your energy field.

» Integrity exists between your personality and your soul.

» Integrity exists between your human and your Creator.

» Integrity exists between all of your relationships.

» There is integrity between your intentions and your actions.

Within spiritual aspirants, it is very common to find a lack of integrity between the energy bodies. For instance, people can express from a highly developed spiritual body or mental body, yet remain highly polarized in the emotions.

In phases of divine embodiment, you are working towards the level of integrity in which your entire energy, the physical, emotional, mental and spiritual bodies, are unified and working synergistically. Your thoughts match your feelings; your feelings match your actions. You 'walk your talk' in every way.

Through the quality of integrity, you create life reflections that mirror this holistic blending. This is true power!

In whatever way you see yourself; you will likewise see the world. If you are separated and disconnected within, this will be your perception of the outside world. If you are angry with yourself, you will be angry at the world. If you have beliefs that are divisive, you will see a divided world. If you have inner conflict, outer chaos will ensue.

If you are one with your totality, perceiving yourself and your creator as unified and working together, your life will function holistically and with a high degree of sustainability. You will experience a reality that is peaceful and purposeful and one that expresses abundance on every level of your life.

This is the truer meaning of divine embodiment. You operate from integrity, whole and undivided with yourself and your source.

FOUNDATIONAL PILLAR #4:
PRESENCE

The fourth foundational pillar to divine embodiment is presence, which is a grounded state of pure awareness.

Presence is your natural state. This means that you are fully present and centered. You are free from regretful thoughts, petty nuisances and future worries.

As an incarnated human, you are an aspect of God awareness and an individualized expression of your total one self. You exist now, only in this now moment. This moment is your only home, past, present and future combined.

The embodiment of your Divine Presence requires a state of consciousness that is coherently connected in the space of now. The present moment is where all manifestation occurs. Everything is reflecting the answers to you right now.

'Now' is the only experiential space in which you actually do exist. When you start leaning back and forth from now into future time or from now into past time, just know that you are removing yourself from the purity of your Divine Presence. Then, all that you want to create and manifest for yourself cannot happen because you are not at home.

Free yourself from the mind that wants to define reality through the past or the future. Things start to get really aligned when you hold clear definitions of who you are from the present moment. 'Now' is where you exist. 'Now' is the real.

How often do we hurry through something, just to get to another something? Often, we rush ourselves to get it done and quite possibly skip over some mighty powerful reflections along the way.

Finishing the project is really not the ultimate goal. Experiencing yourself as the project, in all of its phases, is. The gifts come from the present moment. There is the saying that "the journey is the destination". This cannot be truer.

The bottom line is that life is all about experience and the wisdom gained from that direct experience.

To be divinely embodied, we are poised, grounded and present. This is where we find all of the hidden meanings of nature, our greater abilities, new perception and all next steps. This is how the Divine Presence communicates with us… in the eternal moment!

When we live our life purely in the present moment, we free the mind from the trappings of unpleasant past experiences. The past has served its purpose, leaving us with masterful wisdom gleaned through the direct experience.

To identify with ourselves according to what happened in the past is an illusion because we are no longer that person anymore We are who we are in the now. We have hopefully learned from the past and have already moved on by shifting into another expression.

We must also be careful about attaching to overactive thoughts about the future. The future is created from what we are doing right now.

Of course, we can plan and have general ideas about where we want to go. This is referring to the stress that creeps in when we are constantly concerned about and projecting our energy into a speculated future. This only increases the likelihood that our worries will become a manifested reality.

Presence is the alchemical state. Train yourself to constantly return your self to be fully present, with a calm and empty mind. Keep practicing emptiness while sustaining your awareness upon the supreme source in your life and the grace of its power to carry and sustain you at all times.

Surrendering to emptiness is really surrendering to be your natural self. This means to always be true to the authentic you. You are opening up, in total vulnerability, to the understanding that you are created in the image of the Infinite. Therefore, live your true and most natural self always.

When you are your natural, most authentic self, you will recognize the conflict-free zone of being perfectly centered in abundant life energy.

SHINING FROM YOUR CORE

In this activity of divine embodiment, we are consciously unifying with our great spiritual Presence to become holistically integrated. Whereas before, our spiritual energy may have been hidden, or perceived as separate and even disregarded completely.

It is very common amongst those who are awakening to their greater light to have highly developed spiritual awareness, yet with scattered energy and a lack of focus. There are often energetic fractures in the emotional body, or the mental field, which then brings distortions and health challenges to the physical body.

It is very challenging to accomplish high levels of spiritual integration without the needed balance in the emotional or mental body fields. This is especially true when we are downtrodden against the self, or forcing our way through life, scurrying here and there without the presence of mind that sustains its centeredness.

By placing high priority on building a strong foundation to your spiritual path, any incongruity and imbalance can be greatly lessened. The primary objective is to bring your thoughts, feelings and actions, into resonance with your sacred intent.

The mind thinks the intention. The heart feels it deeply. Your actions speak it loud and clear. You talk your walk. You walk your talk. Your actions match your empowered attitude.

There is no more hiding your amazing spiritual essence!

When your pillars of embodiment are strong and stable...
When you constantly validate the self...
When you operate from full integrity...
When you are centered and present in every moment...

... then wow, you can really shine your light.

We are focusing upon the exquisite state of divine embodiment to enrich and improve the quality of daily life. We are doing this to finally eliminate all suffering and conflict from our lives.

Embodying our greater light will help us to walk in confidence and to be self-assured, with full integrity from the inside out.

Most importantly, we are healing our inner divide and neutralizing the extremes of human polarity. This greatly elevates our vibrational presence and ability to be of tremendous influence to all those around us.

Learn to pause often to just listen, really listen to what is going on around you. Step back and zoom out to be the observer of your life.

Ask yourself,

How am I framing up my life?
Am I validating my self or discounting my self?
Am I walking my talk?
Am I intimately connecting to my Creator?
Do I feel blessed?

Your Divine Presence is always communicating with you, but you have to be still enough to hear and still enough to observe the reflected messages. You also have to be extra careful that you do not discount the self or devalue what is being gifted.

Remember, how you see yourself is how you will see the world. If you are with scattered energy, you will experience a chaotic world. On the other hand, if you keep your focus upon your greater light, you will see a greater, more purposeful plan unfolding.

All is in absolute perfection.

"*Through the internalization of my consciousness, I can shift beyond the human senses and tap into the blissful tone of Divine Presence reverberating through every particle of my body.*"

EVOLVING BEYOND THE
HUMAN SENSES

S ince birth, our consciousness has been trained to perceive through the five corporeal senses. We naturally validate our existence through the physical means of this tactile sensory mechanism.

Our culture and entire societal system is designed to stimulate these senses in every way imaginable. This has locked us up into a sensory driven mind-set consumed with the passing of judgments and categorizing things from their outer appearances.

This makes it quite challenging to tap into the more subtle dimensions of truth that exist just beyond the range of our conditioned perception. We are unaware of them because our minds are not consciously vibrating to perceive any differently.

When sensory perceptions vibrate their pleasures within the body, we are drawn into deep and tenacious attachment to these unique sensations and temporary comforts. Indeed, it is an exquisite experience to be a human. Yet, dependency *only* upon our physical senses keeps us bound up inside a box of limits and distortions.

With our attention constantly placed upon the needs, wants and desires of the physical senses, detecting any other potential reality is nearly impossible. The nature of what we see around us is no more than a thought process projected from our programmed beliefs.

We can now scientifically prove that everything that is perceived through the human senses is really an illusion. Physical reality is not what it appears to be. It is purely a frequency of vibration. We can only outwardly see what is also vibrating at a resonant frequency.

We are now removing the convincing lens of perception that locks us into the loops of conditioned belief. Most limitations exist because of all the materialized appearances that we regard as real. Physical reality is only what we perceive of it.

Outer reality always reflects the inner reality and the perceptions that are held within the consciousness. We are only projecting this experience called physical reality.

With billions of people living together on the same planet, we are living in each other's projections of consciousness as well. This makes it extremely challenging to break free of the patterned dilemma of the limited sensory perception.

The vast majority of us have been taught to perceive physical reality as being solid and this is the only way it could be. It has served us to believe this way. Yet now, the collective human soul is yearning to experience something different. Hence, we are quickly evolving and quickly discovering a more limitless way to thrive in the human experience.

When our definitions about life change, then the reality mirror of that life experience also changes.

The truth is, there are many realities. This is evidenced by our meditative visions, dream excursions, out of body experiences and other seeming paranormal occurrences that go far beyond what the eyes can see. It is in the more subtle realms of energy that a wealth of information exists and can be accessed.

To embody our Divine Presence, we must move off of the playing field that is sustained by the sensory driven perceptual distortion of "what you see is what you get". As long as we are being guided by what our human senses are reading to the brain, we will remain blocked to the subtle messaging coming in from our vaster self.

In the transition we are making, we are learning how to live from multidimensional perception. This far-reaching and more intelligent mindset draws to us expansive opportunities and experiences of a more limitless nature.

This can only happen when our brain is unified with our truer brain of brilliance, the higher mind aspect of the self. It is then that mastermind energy can be channeled through the faculty of the human brain to express higher patterns of thought and feeling.

This phase of expanding sensory perception is likened to an inner brain awakening that develops us as a channel for the higher mind to express more fully, and more purely.

This might out picture as the unfailing voice of intuition that comes in so strong and so clear that there is no waiver of doubt.

This vibrational alignment also increases experiences of positive synchronicity in daily engagement that mirror your exact intentions.

You might find yourself pausing more often when making decisions. There is greater need to consult with your inner feelings, or to enter into meditation, to be at one with the "inner eye" of vision.

There can be a tendency to even wait on a decision until you receive the download of higher messaging, or to be given that unmistakable inner prompting to proceed in a certain way.

These are great examples of being in communication with your higher self, the Divine Presence of your life. This can be perceived as that aspect of brilliance that lives with you at all times as the voice of conscience. It has always been there like a guardian angel guiding you like a beacon, and awakening you from the deep slumber of forgetfulness.

When you can authentically make contact with and cohere to the channel of the vaster self, expanded truths are revealed. You become a 'knower'. This is when you can live your life governed by providence, the direct revelation of Divine Presence expressing through the human form.

To realize this level of divine embodiment, the awareness vibrates above the matter-tuned human senses. The perceptions are turned inwards to reveal the truer reality hidden behind the outer appearance.

Through the internalization of the consciousness, you can shift beyond the human senses and tap into the blissful tone of Divine Presence reverberating through every particle of your body. This is why meditation and intimate communion is so beneficial to your enduring phases of self-realization.

In truth, you are pure awareness temporarily inhabiting a human body in order to develop your consciousness while under the illusory veils.

The physical body is like a virtual reality suit that converts everything you see, hear, touch, taste and smell into electrical impulses that formulate perceptions from inside the brain. These perceptions help you to function in a dense vibrational reality.

In your consciousness shift, you are not leaving or disregarding the human senses, but instead, expanding your sensory perception to function from more dimensions of awareness. You are developing multi-dimensional sight. This level of expanded perception brings you closer to your ultimate freedom from the human conditioning.

Liberation into expanded sensory perception is actualized by learning how to expand into the formless, not bound by rigidity or the walls of separation. The formless is the field of pure potentiality from where all creations spring forth.

From this greater alignment, you can tap into the energy *behind* physical reality, the immanent force guiding everything in the universe into appropriate action.

PERCEIVE FROM THE BIGGER PICTURE

We can gracefully evolve into the higher senses as we embrace more expansive views. This means to consistently regard the bigger picture.

Keep your awareness on the one truth that your Divine Presence is always communicating with you. Everything is perfectly unfolding and is divinely orchestrated for your soul path of evolution. There is no way that you can make a mistake.

This way of thinking gives a new sense of timeless wisdom, which alchemizes a permanent shift in your awareness and entire life.

Life is all about perception. What one person sees as true and real for them may be completely different from what another person sees. Yet, there are always connecting dots between one idea to the next, between one situation and another, between all of the different dimensions of awareness.

It is impossible to see what is really happening on all levels of outplay and the incredible interweaving that is taking place behind the scenes. Yet, snap judgments and instant assessments are constantly being made about people, situations and events. This only brings the viewpoint into a very shallow, false perception.

Because of life's quick pace in the emotion and ego driven world that we live, it is easy to become blind to the rhythms of divine orchestration and the higher meanings of life.

To align with the bigger picture, always consider the underlying harmony and guiding rhythms that is moving all life perfectly and according to a more influential Divine Will. We want to constantly acknowledge the 'unity in diversity' that links everyone and everything to each other.

This is why the best stance to take, in any situation, is neutrality from a compassionate heart. Void of the polarized judgments and charging opinion, this stills the mind to gently open into a more expansive view.

STILLING THE MIND

Stillness in the mind is highly beneficial to our phases of expanded sensory perception. This can be cultivated through meditation, yoga, qigong and other practices that guide you into deep peace and conscious communion with your source of life.

When the awareness is interiorized, the entrance is found more easily into the purity of one's divine essence. From the inner quietude, you can more easily reach into the deep vibrational resonance of peace that is at your core.

As you journey further into states of internal stillness, it becomes easier to release yourself beyond the boundaries of the physical senses.

It is from the stillness that you are gifted with the sight to see beyond the form, where there is no more identity to the human; only to spirit and the holy vibration that you are.

Through the quietude, it is much easier to become one with the energy behind the life, behind the form, behind the thought. You can learn to experience your being, not through the human senses, but as pure awareness itself.

With all that is in great shift and change in our evolving world, there is great need to harness and focus any scattered energy.

Practices that continually ground your energy into your center point are essential.

Learn to constantly observe where the attention is and to be fully present with every thought, action and conversation. When speaking, choose words that blend the self with the higher mind and the greater aspect of your being.

BUILD SENSORY SENSITIVITY

Another way to expand your sensory capability is to build sensitivity to your Divine Presence.

Energetic sensitivity is necessary in order to receive and interpret incoming messages from your higher mind. When this upgraded level of sensitivity is developed, you become a magnet for spiritual ideas and concepts. You learn how to interpret what has been energetically impressed into your auric field.

When your sensitivity to subtle vibration is developed, you become likened to a finely tuned sensory instrument with an ability to positively influence others from your increasing awareness.

This means that the perceptual capability has expanded beyond the realm of the human senses and is able to detect the finer, subtler vibratory fields. The human senses are bridged and working in collaboration with a more sophisticated sensory faculty that receives impressions from divine mind.

Dependency is not solely upon the outer appearance, but also with a channel of attunement that goes beyond the cognizing intellect. This is an expanded brain capacity that can interpret information through insightful spiritual knowledge.

This knowledge comes to you in many ways including the channel of intuition, inner vision and imagination, or simply through your knowing mind.

These divinely attuned capabilities assist us to see beyond the form and to translate our environment from a completely different feedback system. Rather than giving credence to what we are receiving from the outside in, we place greater value with information that comes from the inside out.

This level of expanded sense perception develops in numerous ways and is a very unique experience for each and every person. Some people are born with this gift while others are naturally sensitive to subtle vibration. The majority of people have to develop it in a conscious way and to give that focus a high priority in life.

This development quickens when we start opening the consciousness locks that keep us confined to limited programming. The more that the perception can bend and flex, the more that the vision opens to see beyond the form and beyond the body bound senses.

Development of sensory sensitivity is a phased process that involves raising your vibration to elevate above mass consensus realities.

This begins with deep purification of the physical body. There is required surrendering of the ego and the controlling human tendency. Polarized emotional triggers and reactions must also be neutralized so that your reality can reflect coherence and stability.

The faculties of the higher senses start to noticeably develop when you are mentally calm, emotionally stable and have cultivated a deep sense of inner peace.

The dependency upon rationale and logic must loosen up so that you can perceive into the subtler realms that lie just beyond the material appearances. Through this flexibility, your human senses naturally bridge to the more refined sensory mechanism that relies upon acute sensitivity.

These higher senses are all interrelated; just like the human senses. They afford you a brand new way to observe and communicate from many dimensions of awareness.

You are not only thinking and projecting, but also channeling and intuiting. You are truly like a sensory instrument that attracts and radiates, impresses and transforms.

This is very exciting development!

If you are interested to delve more deeply into this subject matter, consider enrolling into Skillsets of Evolution. This is a training program to assist development of your greater sensory abilities such as intuition, telepathy, magnetism, omnipresence and spiritual radiation. Course information can be found at IAMAvatar.org.

"I am empowered by a greatly expanded perception that brings through information from the impalpable and the invisible."

OPENING THE CHANNELS TO
HIGHER KNOWLEDGE

A t a special moment along the spiritual path, we come to gratefully realize that the only meaningful desire in life is to serve and to be a positive influence upon others.

For many spiritual aspirants, one of the greatest motivators is to help others awaken and transform. This comes with considerable desire to serve as a channel for the intervening forces of benevolent grace that are influencing our planetary evolution.

This is exactly the level of empowerment that this book inspires. It is encouraging deeper phases of spiritual integration so that highest levels of love, wisdom and empowered service can be creatively expressed through the human vessel.

To accomplish this intention, it is imperative to expand our sensory abilities. This regards one's perceptual capability and how incoming information is translated. We must learn how to interpret information beyond the realm of the physical dimension and beyond the tangibility of the human experience.

It is like re-molding the self into a sort of multi-pronged, walking antennae, constantly receiving and transmitting messages from Spirit.

The human senses are bridged and working in collaboration with a more sophisticated sensory faculty that receives impressions directly from the higher mind. Dependence is not *only* upon the brain, but also with a channel of attunement that functions outside of the cognizing intellect.

This is referring to an expanded brain capacity that can interpret information through gnosis, or insightful spiritual knowledge. This is a level of intelligence that comes as a result of the personal experience, not merely from learned concepts, beliefs, or theories.

A different feedback system is used to interpret and translate information. The difference is that one's beliefs are no longer created by what is perceived from the outside in. Instead, personal truth is cultivated from sensory information coming from the inside out.

Herein lies the crux of this subject matter. We are learning how to interpret sensory information from the inside out.

This occurs most easily once the channels to the greater aspects of self are open and flowing. This is all about building the bridge, which unifies the human mind with the higher mind. This bridging requires activation and subsequent expansion of the energetic pathways of sensory interpretation.

With open channels, we are able to smoothly navigate life through new mental faculties, including the unfailing voice of intuition. The pineal gland starts to function as a multidimensional antenna. We are inspired through the ethereal waves of spiritual telepathy and move within the rhythms of positive synchronicity.

It feels like we are becoming a different breed as we start sensing energy fields upon instinct, just like an animal.

This level of expanded sense perception develops in numerous ways and is a very unique experience for each and every person.

Some people are even born with this gift and are naturally sensitive to the subtle realms. Other people have to develop it in a conscious way and to give that focus a high priority in life.

No matter what method or spiritual practice is used to support the sensory upgrade, the actualization requires opening of the often-dormant channels that, once activated, connect us directly to our higher mind.

We learn how to shift the dependency from solely upon the brain's intellect and into pure gnosis. The basis of the insightful gnostic expression is an unfolding inclusiveness, an expanding perception that can vision far beyond the realm of our conditioned brain and its sensory programming.

There is no doubt or insecurity that enters upon this screen of reality. This level of intelligence unites. It is wholly concerned with the principles of oneness and the interconnectivity of all life.

No matter how smart we are at the human level, we simply cannot advance our consciousness through the brain's intellect alone. It occurs through the influence of our Divine Presence, the higher mind intelligence that enters into us as pure knowing.

To sincerely comprehend the intrinsic nature of this, let's make the distinction between the brain's intellect and higher mind intelligence.

Through the intellect of a healthy person, the brain has been well developed with many facts and can operate accurately in a variety of mental functions. While useful in traditional modes of learning, the brain's intellect cannot fully grasp the finer vibrational perceptions, which have their origin in unified awareness.

In other words, true unity cannot be actualized through reasoning, logic or concrete thinking.

Alternatively, one who has true intelligence, channeled through the faculty of the higher mind, has a keen ability to know the difference between the real and the unreal. This intelligence is fully aware of the illusions of life and can perceive the truths that are covered up by these same illusions.

For most people, the real dilemma is the conditioned consciousness, which has been tenaciously trained to perceive experiences through the five human senses, dominated by concrete thinking.

This has prevented us from tapping into other dimensions of awareness that exist just beyond the range of our normal perception. We are unaware of them because our minds are not consciously vibrating at these higher levels.

A way to effectively expand the sensory perception is to bridge and marry the brain's cognition with divine knowing. Divine knowing is a level of wisdom that comes as a result of the intuitive process of truly knowing yourself. To know yourself at the deepest level is to simultaneously know and experience your great Divine Presence revealing in your life.

This is why a great deal of emphasis throughout this book is placed on how to connect and thrive with your higher mind and with your great Divine Presence.

The assimilation of pure knowledge channeled from the Divine Presence supersedes the human intellect through a finely tuned intuition and the living of life through a more supreme thought system.

When our thoughts and feelings are realigned and orienting to this more supreme way to interpret, we start remembering. We begin anchoring into our physical reality what we already know in the expanded versions of the self.

YOUR IMAGE AND LIKENESS

There are many influential spiritual truths that apply to our phases of new thought unification. One of these is the metaphysical principle of "correspondence", which speaks to the mirror-image relationship between all that exists in the cosmos.

It shares that all things in the universe are infinitely interconnected. No matter what form of energy is presenting itself, everything is representing the larger whole.

This idea expresses that humans are made in the image and likeness of the one original Creator of everything, at the most macro level. All forms of life are birthed from this one primary source.

Everything that occurs in life is a reflection and a stepped down version of a greater flow of energy. Essentially, there is only one consciousness at play. We are made in its image and likeness.

To evolve our perception, the one belief that must disintegrate concerns the idea that the consciousness is something that is located inside our physical body, perhaps somewhere in the brain.

We are much, much bigger than this! Our consciousness actually exists outside of the physical body, even outside of this Earthly dimension. Our consciousness is like a wave in the infinite ocean of universal awareness.

It can be quite mind boggling to try and grasp the idea that you are the entire universe and one small fragment of your consciousness is experiencing itself in the form of a human being. Contemplate this truth deeply. Consider that your unique consciousness existed before you were born, that it has always existed and always will exist.

We are still baffled by these ideas but one thing is for certain. Our consciousness is neither a by-product of brain chemistry nor the result of an inherited genetic code.

As thinking humans, we are endowed with a blueprint of supreme intelligence. It is encoded in every one of our cells. The human brain and its perceptual faculties can be retrained to serve in a brand new way; as a receiving station and channel for a more intelligent language of light.

In the transition that you are making, you are learning how to live from a greatly expanded perception that brings through information from the impalpable and the invisible. This can only happen when your brain is unified with our truer brain of brilliance, the higher mind aspect of your vast constitution.

WHAT IS THE HIGHER MIND?

The term, higher mind, is referenced quite a bit in this content. 'Higher mind' is used to mean that part of the higher mental body that connects and links the human soul to the dimension of unified awareness.

The higher mental body is a part of a person's auric field together with other energetic layers such as the emotional body and etheric body. The mental body is the vehicle of expression for the thinking human intelligence. It holds your thoughts, perceptions and mental processes.

A person with a healthy mental body can focus the consciousness easily with clear thought processes. It is from mental stability that the intelligence of Divine Presence can influence a person's thinking.

The mental body can also be influenced by the over dominant human ego, and become stagnated through built up energetic blocks and negative feedback. This is why deep purification of the personality's ego is extremely important to consciousness advancement. It is only through a stable and humble mind that the channels to the higher mind open more easily.

CONCRETE VERSUS ABSTRACT THINKING

It is helpful to reflect upon the dominant pathways through which the human mind expresses.

We have a lower concrete mind and a higher spiritual, or abstract mind. These two aspects of the mind enable us to exist and communicate in both the physical dimension and in ethereal realities.

Abstract thinking is a creative mindset that contemplates ideas that are both tangible and intangible. It is more conceptual and takes into consideration a bigger picture, knowing that there may be more than one meaning for something. The broader significance of ideas and information is considered rather than just the outward appearances.

Conversely, concrete thinking just regards the facts and what can be seen. It is based upon tangibility and what is presenting itself as proven evidence. It looks at things literally. Concrete thinkers like to follow instructions and have detailed plans. There is challenge to 'read between the lines' and to perceive energetic interconnectivity.

For example, think about a person meditating. An abstract thinker would consider if this person is alone or in a group, whether this person is sitting, lying down, inside or outdoors, in the silence or listening to music, etc. A concrete thinker would simply think of a person meditating.

We use both concrete and abstract reasoning at different times and in different situations. It would be very challenging to get through life relying on only one way of thinking. For most people, however, one type of thinking dominates.

To open the channels into higher knowledge and move beyond the brain's intellect, it is helpful to cultivate an ability to think in abstract fluidity. To improve abstract thinking, we must learn how to perceive the bigger picture. This expanded viewpoint constantly reflects upon the multiple meanings and inherent unity of life's reflections.

When focused in the intelligence of the abstract mind, this level of consciousness is like a doorway, which provides access to a blended union with the higher mind. The higher mind is greatly influenced by the Divine Presence, our greater aspect that truly runs the show.

Again, your Divine Presence is the non-physical component of yourself that acts as a conduit to all other dimensional aspects of yourself. It is the intermediary that distills information from the spiritual realms in a way that you, the personality, can understand.

Once the mind and emotions are stable, this benevolent influence can work in collaboration with the personality. It can help reorient the physical brain and entire consciousness to function through high states of coherence.

Through the higher mind, your Divine Presence can enable you to make decisions with utmost clarity and to know the truth, apart from any rationalization. This inner guidance can speak and write through you without the use of the methodical brain, as you have been accustomed.

When you can authentically make contact with and cohere to the channel of the vaster self, expanded truths are revealed. You become a 'knower'. This is when you can live your life governed by providence, the direct revelation of Divine Presence expressing through your form.

This entire book is sharing numerous ways on how to do this. It has previously shared about:

» Building a new thought structure

» Perceiving through Divine Principle

» Neutralizing emotional polarity

» Transcending the ego

» Expanding sensory perception

» Following your inspiration

We have also learned the importance of building a very strong and stable foundation in order to elevate into our greater expression.

We are now going to zero in on opening the channels to higher knowledge. Once these pathways are created, it much easier for your Divine Presence to effectively communicate through you, as its human channel.

This is how it was intended to work. The purpose of our human brain and its driving ego is to purely and humbly serve as a receiving station for the language of our higher self of the light.

OPENING THE CHANNELS

Inherent within us are certain mental faculties designed to bridge our human mind into the expanded realms of the multi-dimension.

These divinely attuned instruments assist us to see beyond the form and to interpret our environment from a completely different feedback mechanism.

For example, this new and upgraded feedback can express through the pathways of the intuition, precognition, spiritual telepathy, inner vision and magnetic radiance.

These types of higher sensory abilities develop as a result of your advancing spiritual path and arduous efforts to purify the human conditioning.

Once purified enough, three primary channels are among the first to organically come online, which guide us into deepening communion with our higher mind.

THE CHANNEL OF ATTUNEMENT

There is a particular ability that is absolutely essential to expand into the higher senses. This is the state of being attuned, 'in tune', with your higher mind.

Your higher mind functions like a translator. It relays higher dimensional information to you in a way that it can be deciphered and applied. What you receive and how you receive it is directly linked to your phase of evolutionary development. The more that you perceive from the higher senses, the more that greater truths will be revealed.

To be in attunement means to be in symphony with something. In this case, you are in symphony with your greater intelligence. This brings on a feeling of being 'at one'. Your attuned mind is aware of another, more influential consciousness that is always there in the background of everything, constantly impressing.

When the channel of attunement is developed, any dispersing mental energy is trained to return to the harmonic rhythm of single eye focus. The personality is stabilized with balanced mental and emotional energy.

Through this level of attunement, you can co-create and magnetize all that you need and require because you are living through the guidance of your higher mind.

Developed attunement usually results from a dedicated spiritual practice and constant purification of the physical, emotional, mental and spiritual energy bodies from which we function.

Cultivating an ability to focus and concentrate is also a golden key. This is why meditation, yoga and mind-body exercises are encouraged, especially those that help focus the intention and bring us into deep spiritual awareness and alignment.

THE CHANNEL OF THE MORPHOGENETIC
ANTAHKARANA

Another important channel that assists us into the higher senses and pristine alignment with our higher mind is what is called the morphogenetic antahkarana.

Antahkarana is an ancient Sanskrit word that means the totality of two levels of mind. This can simply be regarded as a sacred bridge that connects the lower mind with the higher mind. Yet, in no way is this to be understood linearly.

In truth, the antahkarana connects to many aspects of our vaster self, including all dimensions of awareness, timelines and parallel realities that we simultaneously exist within. This bridging mechanism is part of our personal morphogenetic field architecture, which connects our entire human hologram to all that exists.

The term, morphogenetic field, identifies and guides the way that our human consciousness develops. It does this through stored memory-based encoding. All conscious creation, from micro to macro, is manifested through these imprinting field templates. Likewise, layers of morphogenetic imprints exist around each person's energy body.

This blueprint is known as our personal morphogenetic field. Holographic in nature, this field expands to exist at every level and dimension we exist within, from Earth to the cosmos.

The developing antahkarana is part of our personal morphogenetic field, as are the higher chakra energy centers that help bridge our awareness to expanding levels of consciousness. We are placing focus on activating more of the antahkarana bridge that connects to and receives information from the higher mind.

The emphasis is on maturation of the human heart and the human mind as a fused entity. This synthesized pathway opens us up as a multi-faceted receiving channel. The wise and compassionate heart and the mind's intelligent awareness are joined and operate as a singular entity.

When evolved in this way, an important bridge is built that unifies the human heart-mind with the higher mental body. This gives direct access to the intelligence of Divine Presence, linking the two levels of mind intelligence in collaboration.

The building of this intertwined frequency helps us to be consciously responsive to impressions from our higher mind and the language of light.

To build and strengthen this bridging cohesion, we are essentially merging and synthesizing the energy that emanates from our heart, as a compassionate and loving heart, together with our throat and its ability to express coherent ideas.

This stream of energy joins up with our mind as the center of spiritual intelligence. This is commonly visualized as an intertwining cord of energy that intertwines the energy of the heart, the throat and the pineal gland.

As a result of soulful and aligned thought, this bridge of union, from human mind to higher mind, is eventually built. It is fortified by a sincere desire to be of service to others.

Note: The building of the antahkarana is also strengthened through your attunement to the collected enlightened mind, of which you are an integral part. When there is genuine coherence to this unified luminosity, the brain rewires itself to be a receiver of the group intelligence, comprising the minds of all people who are similarly tuned.

With great numbers of people operating in this way, a sustaining matrix of telepathic communication develops.

THE CHANNEL OF THE PINEAL GATEWAY

Another important channel into expanding sensory perception involves the opening of the pineal gland's dimensional gateway.

An open and activating pineal gland provides the springboard for optimal spiritual development.

The power of attunement with the pineal gland opens the visionary channels of perception and connects you to the higher mind. When this channel is opened, the light of knowledge surges through your pineal gland to give valuable information to the rest of your biological template. You quickly learn how to rhythmically move with the voice of the greater conscience.

Briefly, the pineal gland is part of the endocrine system living at the center of your brain. Commonly called the third eye, this multifaceted gland is shaped like a tiny pinecone, no larger than the size of very small raison.

Its role as a light receptor is to translate incoming frequencies of light so that encoded messages can be delivered through the hormonal pathways and passing on instructions for bodily functions.

With its central hormone, melatonin, the pineal gland regulates the biological rhythms of the body. It works in harmony with the hypothalamus gland, which directs your sleep cycles plus other activities such as thirst, hunger, sexual desire and the biological clock. It also orchestrates your endocrine and nervous systems.

What is most interesting is that natural light is what activates this special gland. When turned on, the pineal gland becomes involved with helping us reach into higher states of consciousness.

Bolstered by its naturally producing spirit molecule DMT, or dimethyltryptamine, the pineal gland is the doorway through which we exit linear construct. It moves us beyond the human intellect and into an expanded brain capacity that perceives from a more powerful 'knowing' mind.

Human beings were intended to be visionaries of great sensitivity and able to tap into information from other dimensional frequencies. Activating and caring for the pineal gland is essential for those wanting to develop multidimensional perception. As such, we need to give high priority to this pivotal center of our evolving potential. When the pineal gland is fully operational, we are able to remain in a visionary state most of the time.

The pineal gland truly is our gateway into other dimensions of consciousness. Thus, it needs to be cared for and nurtured back to its intended design to allow access into our higher potentials.

The more you practice using your pineal gland to see beyond the matter dimension, the stronger it gets. As your pineal gland becomes stronger and more active, your ability to access information from the higher mind will dramatically increase.

Following is an excerpt from my book, Morphogenesis & The Skillsets of Evolution. It gives a brief, basic summary on some of the ways to nurture and stimulate the pineal gland for optimal functioning.

GIVING SUPPORT TO THE PINEAL GLAND

The pineal gland has lost its original function as a spiritual antenna due to the density of human consciousness, characterized by divisive tendencies and toxic thoughts. This dormancy is now a genetic imprint.

As a race, we are functioning without our capacity 'to know'. Calcification of the pineal gland is constantly being reinforced by our culture and from a whole host of artificial dependencies. Artificial is the key word.

The effect of inorganic substances and environmental toxins, that both surround us and get inside our bodies, has contributed to this resulting calcification.

An example of these harmful substances includes fluoride chemicals found in public water systems and toothpaste, environmental toxins, plus hormones, additives, sugars and artificial sweeteners added to our foods. High concentrations of radiation from our cell phones is also hailed as harmful to the structures of the brain.

The effect of smoke inhalation and alcohol are major detriments to a highly activated pineal gland. If you want to be in your most tip top shape on all levels, remove any and all smoking habits and excessive drinking. This cannot be emphasized enough. Smoke and alcohol dull the brain cells, clog the receiving channels and cause fracturing in your crystalline circuitry.

Detoxification is an essential place to start if we want to champion our full spiritual capabilities. We want pineal glands that are healthy, strong and expanding and then giving that same reflection to the nervous and endocrine systems.

For optimal functioning of the third eye, I suggest an approach that focuses on the three main areas of:

1. Detoxification
2. Strengthening
3. Expansion

This is the three-prong strategy that I have used and continue to address, all the days of my life, as I place myself in service to the Divine. I enjoy great health and am constantly inspired. I am also quite intense in my spiritual life so take what resonates for you and go at your own pace.

THOUGHTS

The single most important qualifier to this subject matter is the ability to maintain thoughts that match your highest preferences in life. The more limited and negative that we are in our thoughts, the more calcified the pineal gland becomes, preventing access through this spiritual portal.

It goes without saying that your thoughts, feelings and actions are the most important considerations to any type of pineal strengthening program.

Your pineal gland produces a number of chemicals and hormones that bring on joy, happiness, bliss, restfulness and inspiration. These states give great support to the pineal pathways that send messages to the rest of your body. If you are not feeling harmonious, this is your cue to pause and contemplate so that the core cause of low feelings can be shifted.

A lack of proper attention upon what we are allowing ourselves to be exposed to, such as runaway negative thoughts and emotion, will shut us down from accessing our higher mind.

ELIMINATE ALL SOURCES OF FLUORIDE

To restore the pineal gland; the one strategy we are all familiar with is to eliminate sources of fluoride. This chemical has proven to be a high risk factor associated with calcification because it collects in extremely high amounts in this glandular center.

Fluoride is an endocrine disruptor that not only adversely affects the pineal gland but also many other structures and functions in the body, including the bones, brain, thyroid and blood. Overexposure to fluoride decreases melatonin production and destabilizes your body's mineral balance. This causes your pineal gland to calcify very quickly.

There are many additional sources of fluoride, other than just what is found in public water systems. Many commercial toothpaste companies add fluoride to their products. Other sources include processed foods made with fluoridated water, fluoride-containing pesticides, bottled teas, fluorinated pharmaceuticals, teflon pans and even mechanically deboned chicken. Enough said.

DETOX HEAVY METALS
(AND OTHER INVADERS)

Heavy metals can accumulate in the body and greatly impact our health and organ functioning. These metals are very harmful to your expansion into multidimensional sensitivity and can be highly destructive to the brain. The pineal gland is particularly susceptible to heavy metals because it is not protected by the body's blood-brain barrier system and has a very high blood perfusion rate.

The heavy metals most commonly associated with pineal poisoning are lead, mercury, aluminum and arsenic. Heavy metal poisoning may occur as a result of air or water pollution, inhaling lead-based paint fumes, industrial exposure, and more commonly those which are found in some foods, medicines, vaccines, amalgam tooth fillings, cosmetics, deodorants, cooking pans, colorants, additives, toxic chemicals, pesticides... the list is very long.

If you suspect that you have heavy metals in your system, do some good research and proper testing so that a personal detox program can be created that is specific to you. A lot of this is really about making the necessary lifestyle changes that effectively keep you in detox and alkalizing mode all of the time.

Heavy metals don't easily leave the body unless specific steps are taken to remove them. One of the things I have done was to get my mercury fillings replaced. I have also done a lot of infrared saunas and ionic footbaths. I often do whole body detox through herbs, food fasting and ingesting a lot of betonite volcanic clay to help pull out those harmful toxins.

Note: This information also applies to many other invaders in the body that wreck havoc on your systems such as parasites, bacteria, fungi, mucous, viruses, chemicals, medications, etcetera.

ALKALINE NUTRITION AND SUPERFOODS

The highest recommendation I can give for keeping your pineal gland happy and thriving is to sustain your body in a high alkaline state. Always consider your pH balance, which is a measure of body acidity. An alkaline diet and plenty of high pH water appears to be my best recipe for sustaining all that I do so intensely in my spiritual development and activation work.

Foods, such as meat, refined sugar, gluten, dairy and processed foods, will often cause the body to over-produce acid if these are consumed on a heavy basis. Your body is designed to function most efficiently with a blood pH balance of at least seven and above. Too much acid in the blood causes imbalances and, eventually, diseases and further calcification of the pineal gland.

Eating a good diet consisting of alkaline foods, such as fresh fruit and vegetables, and clean, energized water, will help maintain your body's natural balance. When you eat processed and acidic food your body has to pull nutrients out of your body's mineral base to neutralize the acidity.

Nutrition is the key to an open and working pineal gland. Really look at everything that you consume and eliminate all processed foods and those that contain anything artificial. Make it your lifestyle to eat organically and select foods that give your body ultimate support.

Following are some great staples to have on hand.

CHLOROPHYLL RICH SUPERFOODS

Chlorophyll is what collects light from the sun to make energy in plants, and it's also what gives plants their beautiful green color. Naturally found in leafy vegetables, it has a host of benefits for the body.

Chlorophyll also has ability to bind and remove toxic heavy metals from your body. It neutralizes germ-causing diseases and is a good source of magnesium that will alkalinize. It's also an anti-oxidant, preventing harmful oxidation in the body.

Consider adding chlorophyll rich superfoods to your diet regimen like spirulina, chlorella, wheatgrass and blue-green algae. These are also pineal detoxifiers and pineal stimulants that are packed with vitamins, minerals and antioxidants. These superfoods help decalcify the pineal gland, increase oxygen levels, repair damaged tissue, and boost your immune system.

LEMONS

Lemons are acidic to the taste, but are alkaline-forming in the body. In fact they are one of the most alkaline-forming foods. They are rich in nutrients and are super cleansing to the body.

I either drink a glass of lemon water every morning or make a morning elixer comprised of high pH water, the juice of one lemon, a dropper full of liquid chlorophyll and a couple capfuls of some apple cider vinegar.

APPLE CIDER VINEGAR

Apple cider vinegar is another one that has a long list of alkalizing health benefits. It supports the digestive system and helps the body detoxify. It is also antibacterial, antiviral and antifungal.

Be sure that the brand you buy is raw, organic and packaged in a glass container.

COCONUT OIL

Saluted as brain food, coconut oil contains a unique combination of fatty acids with powerful medicinal properties. Its greatest benefit may be that it revitalizes the brain and detoxes the pineal gland.

It is said that the medium chain triglycerides found in coconut oil are broken down into ketones by the liver and readily cross the blood-brain barrier to provide instant energy to brain cells.

This food restores neurons, improves nerve function in the brain, and can delay brain aging and memory loss. Studies have actually shown that that the fatty acids in coconut oil supply the right type of energy for the brain cells of Alzheimer's patients to relieve their symptoms.

NATURAL LIGHT SUPPORT

Your pineal gland is light sensitive. Light reflected by the retina stimulates the pineal gland; therefore, it is highly beneficial to be exposed to indirect sunlight on a daily basis.

Wearing sunglasses may not be the best thing for those who desire expanded pineal functioning. We definitely want the natural light reflecting into our eyes.

Sungazing is the practice of staring at the sun during sunrise or sunset. During this time, the light emitted from the sun isn't as strong, making it safer to look directly into it.

Many people who sungaze believe that it is favorable to the eyes and the pineal gland. Scientific studies have confirmed that sunlight can stimulate the pineal gland to secret certain hormones.

ALL FORMS OF MEDITATION

Meditation, chanting, yoga and conscious breathing are all effective ways to activate the pineal gland. Studies have also shown increased pineal gland activity during all forms of sincere meditation. This correlates to the frequency of spiritual experiences that happen during very deep states of inner attunement.

Meditation stimulates development of the interiorized awareness and is a powerful practice to assist your ability to focus and to hold your steadiness in the pure clear spiritual light. Think of meditation as a form of strength training for the pineal gland and a way to condition the mind to be quiet and more receptive to higher states of consciousness.

VISUALIZATION

When you visualize, you are forcing your mind to use your third eye. By doing this, you can stimulate your pineal gland into greater activation. As your pineal gland becomes more active, higher frequencies of energy can flow into your body. This influence can heal your body and awaken other dormant sections of your brain.

The pineal gland truly is our gateway into other dimensions of consciousness. Thus, it needs to be cared for and nurtured back to its intended design to allow us access into our higher potentials.

The more you practice using your pineal gland to see beyond the material world, the stronger it gets. As your pineal gland becomes stronger and more active, your ability to access information from higher frequency fields will increase.

"As divine love is expressed in service to others, I release creation's unlimited storehouse of supply. If I truly love, I cannot help but give. To give is to expand and thus the Law of Love is fulfilled."

SERVING AS
LOVE'S RADIATOR

The influence of divine love upon our sacred sweet Earth is now in phenomenal outplay. Continuous outpourings of this all-embracing energy are catalyzing great shifts in the hearts and minds of people everywhere.

Pouring itself out as benevolent grace, this light of love is permeating into all open channels to bless, to awaken and to transform the human nature.

The current state of world affairs may seem as if we are moving into an opposite direction. All that is uprising is actually the result of this love light that is saturating our world with its transfiguring rays. Naturally, all that is held in distortion is going to eventually purge and buckle.

It can be easy to lose hope during a time of extreme darkness, but rest assured, this is a necessary cycle holding unprecedented possibilities for spiritual transformation and mass scale awakening.

The incoming cosmic light is catalyzing final closure to the age of conflict. Its transcended state of harmony is rising to meet the demands of the hour. The highly transforming radiation is also affecting crucial and progressive alignment within the consciousness of the masses.

It is creating the required opening for universal love to gently enter into the hearts of all people while releasing the energy of goodwill. This is reorienting the collective focus of self-interest to equality and the greater good of all.

It is natural that those with awakened consciousness are the ones helping to carry out this evolutionary divine plan. Cloaked with our mantle of compassion, we are being called in greater numbers to influence a global harmonization and to bring higher understanding to awakening humanity.

PERSONALITY LOVE VERSUS DIVINE LOVE

The actualization of divine love in the awareness is one of the most important initiations that we are taking as an evolving consciousness.

Every phase of our spiritual awakening is highly purposed to help create the ideal inner conditions that allows for the embodiment of Divine Presence and the full expression of this greater love.

To comprehend the significance of divine love, it is helpful to interpret this intelligent energy in terms of a unified field versus the personal self. As we enter into this greater alignment, we choose to be love's willing instruments to help raise and redeem all life upon the Earth.

The very nature of divine love surpasses all description. The following is merely an attempt to do so.

Let's start with the ideas of love from a human perspective.

What is considered as love by the majority of people is not really true love at all but a mixture of the desire to love and the desire to be loved and acknowledged. There is often an over-emphasis to show and evoke sentiment in order to be emotionally comfortable in one's own life.

This type of love is emotionally based, which is often attaching and dependent. It comes from a place of personal need and self-interest. Although illusion, this pseudo love has been a very necessary experience in our life's plan. It has helped us to learn more about the self through dualistic relationships of all types.

We are now progressing beyond personality love and into an expansion of consciousness that realizes the self as a vibrant and powerful center of fundamental, universal love and blessed with an expanded capacity to influence larger numbers of people.

Consider that the love of our Creator is not affectionate, emotional or sentimental. This radiant field of intelligence knows no opposite nor does it come from a place of need. It is a neutralizing, cohesive force and its transforming power is boundless.

Divine love wields the cohesive power that guides the universe, leading and sustaining everything into integration, unity and inclusiveness.

This love is pure intelligence. It naturally liberates. Its wisdom clarifies and impels motive. This brings magnetic attraction into play to produce cohesion. When you are touched by its radiation, it initiates a grand return to your core essence. This results in the unification of consciousness at our level of the human existence.

During phases of spiritual initiation, we are undergo tremendous shifts in our awareness to self-realize our greater self. Essentially, this means to step up in service as part of the potent collective expression of divine love in action.

This level of love is inclusive. It is love for the whole of life, which is a completely different demonstration than the personality's affection for friends, children or a life partner.

We are shifting the perceptual awareness to consistently see and regard the whole of creation. To live just for a select few in our life keeps us in the confines of limiting consciousness.

When we truly embrace the interconnectivity of all of our life's relationships, we flow naturally into unity awareness. We then realize our eternal nature in harmony with the universal codes of God Consciousness.

You will know that the fire of true love is radiating inside you if your love for all people is greater than the love of yourself and of your individual relationships. You do not even think about personal happiness because your focus in life is upon goodwill to others.

You will know when you have reached this level of vibration when you can smile at every person that you confront in your life without passing any thought of judgment. Instead, you look into their eyes and only see the beauty that exists in their soul.

It is through living a humble life, without attachment or dependency upon anything outside of the self, that we make transition into a clear, unimpeded vehicle for the wisdom and generosity of God's love.

The purity of this love gives constantly as its inherent nature, requiring nothing back in return. The expression of divine love through us naturally produces sincere outward compassion and giving.

The basis of this expression is an unfolding inclusiveness; an expanded perception that can vision far beyond the realm of duality programming and ego based thoughtforms.

To behold a more inclusive awareness does not mean that we are required to give up our family or other cherished loved ones. It simply means that our conscious perception now reaches out, beyond the mortal circumference, to truly embrace all of life, equally and without exception.

The love of your Divine Presence is always with you. This love is all giving. Remember this one truth and you will naturally be without self-serving desires. This is because you will know that all of your needs are taken care of at all times. There will be no addictions or compulsions. Greed will vanish. The seeking goes away. The heart opens even wider. The spirit of generosity emerges.

Active service in the spirit of generosity is one of the most significant understandings to realizing the self as part of the benevolent God force.

This is when we come to realize true selflessness. Every activity, including our thoughts, feelings, words and acts, becomes centered upon service and giving.

In this turning point of our evolution, we are motivated by love and love alone to carry out a much greater Will upon the Earth.

It is through love and generosity that we freely share our truths to assist in the global awakening and humanity's transition into unity consciousness.

THE LAW OF LOVE AND GENEROSITY

As more people everywhere want to show integrity in their character, their internal nature begins to harmonize and operate under the influence of the divine principles.

These universal laws are the very foundation stones upon which we are building our new paradigm of coherent and abundant living. These are the same laws or principles by which everything in the universe is governed.

The Law of Generosity is one of the main governing principles to realize an emergence of global unity and peace upon the Earth. The most significant maxim of this illumined era is: "To those who give all, all is given."

As we express divine love in service to others, we release creation's unlimited storehouse of supply. If we truly love, we cannot help but give. To give is to expand and thus the Law of Love is fulfilled.

The purity of our greater love gives constantly as its inherent nature, requiring nothing back in return. With no expectation of return as a result of giving, it is impossible to avoid receiving. The energy is returned to us, amplified, through the natural fulfillment of the law.

As we come to live in greater alignment with these governing principles, all sense of lack evaporates for we humbly know that it is through the act of giving that we shall receive.

There is an infinite supply of abundance available for all. The experience of lack is merely an illusion. Lack consciousness is the result of human attachment to the material plane.

This is why we must endure the challenging phases of soul initiation to squelch the ego and sever the emotional cords of outer dependence. This we must do before realizing our true inheritance and the ability to give selflessly.

To experience true spiritual wealth, is to live first and foremost in the perfect freedom of divine immanence. From this state of liberation, we are vibrating beyond the boundaries of limitation, relinquished of all thoughts of having and needing material things.

The will to serve versus being served keeps the life current flowing through the illumined self. It is when we are fulfilling the needs of others that we open the storehouse of the Divine Presence to flow through us unimpeded.

CHARACTERISTICS OF A TRUE
HUMANITARIAN

The genuine servers who are leading humanity into higher evolution stand as one in group formation, working silently in self-forgetfulness, having already offered up their personality for use by divinity.

They give no thought to the magnitude of their accomplishments and bear no preconceived ideas as to their own value or usefulness. Their attitude is to live and serve, asking nothing for themselves and needing no reward. The act of giving *is* the reward.

These enlightened ones are completely unattached to the results, walking in perfect equanimity as they respond to the needs of the moment. When it comes to real humanitarian service, sincerity is the king of all virtues.

All acts of service are expressed in an effort to magnify the glory of the Divine Presence in everyone, brought forth through a sincere attitude of love and goodwill towards all. True selflessness stems from one who is deeply in love with the sacredness of life.

Second only to sincerity, humility is the next pivotal key to opening the channels to greater levels of service. No task is considered too great or too small.

True servers do not wait for grandiose opportunities to give and serve. They start immediately, giving whatever they can to aide those around them thus adding to the grandeur of love's expression on Earth.

It is through humility and meekness that we are able to serve as effective vessels to radiate the light of love and its transforming grace. We actually become a transforming presence everywhere we go.

You might have already experienced situations where you have positively influenced someone just by your energy presence alone. It may be that this person was triggered when you were around due to the detoxifying affect that can happen when a higher vibrational frequency field meets up with a lower one.

This is to be expected when you advance into greater vibrations of consciousness.

SERVING AS LOVE'S RADIATOR

Your spiritual radiation is a form of vibrational medicine within the unified field of interconnected energy. It is a living remedy empowered by your divine alignment and coherence with the unified field.

When you have reached this stage of conscious evolution, it really does not matter what techniques are employed because they all work. Mistakes cannot be made. You have raised your vibration to the level of being able to shift the energy fields of others through your sacred intention alone. Accomplished results are even more dramatic when there is a willing receiver on the other end.

Whether you are a healer, teacher, business executive or brick-layer, you can radiate divine love in everything that you do. Choose your unique expression and methodology, and thrive! This is how you are being used.

God is in control and you are simply serving as an instrument, according to the highest good of the person or object of your service.

Rather than thinking you must acquire the latest and greatest modalities and resources to have at your disposal, you can choose to leave all of the tools and techniques at the door. You can even modify your approach into a much easier one to conserve energy output.

Once you are able to sustain your vibration with the love of your Divine Presence, your entire energy field naturally becomes a useful channel. The divine flows through you no matter if you serve naked and bare or if you have a large portfolio of accomplishments and state of the art gadgets to assist your mission.

When you are serving as an instrument for your Divine Presence, you are surrounding yourself with love, the greatest power of the universe. From this highly magnetic resonance, you are naturally powerful and invincible.

The metaphysical principle to keep in mind is that higher frequencies always overcome the denser vibrations. Greater is more powerful than the lesser. The whole is more cohesive than the part.

Remain unified and in this divine attunement! You can walk in this world and not be affected by any chaos and negativity.

As a radiating channel of love, you can best assist those who are challenged by what you have *already* overcome. You have the solution encoded in your energy field. It is amazing to observe how those who are attracted to you are the ones who will benefit the most by what you have already healed and activated within yourself.

In your role as love's radiator, you essentially form a bridge between worlds and serve as a guardian of the divine light. In this guardianship, you can sustain and build upon its momentum by consistently and consciously qualifying every thought, word, feeling and action with the power of love.

Everywhere you go, in every handshake, in every hug, in every word, thought, feeling and in every action, you are constantly transferring your imprinting out into the world.

As we maneuver within a hectic, fast paced world, it is often very challenging to keep the consciousness free of anything less than the divine concept. Constant vigilance to self-correct any discordance in your thoughts, feelings and actions is paramount to divine embodiment. This mastery of energy will greatly enhance the quality of radiance from your field.

As we come to truly embody divine love as an evolved collective consciousness, our capacity to serve humanity is significantly amplified. Free of the colorings of the human personality, we are able to intelligently direct love-wisdom into every circumstance to affect instantaneous transformation.

Serving as an instrument of divinity, we love as God loves. We give and keep on giving. We radiate and keep on radiating.

All humanity is a reflection of our one self and the one consciousness of all life. When we give to our neighbor, we are also giving to ourselves.

May supreme kindness and generous action become our natural way of life as we stand united in our power of love.

The true humanitarian spirit is then revealed as a result of our seeing the Divine in every face and every seeming wound of humanity is also considered our own.

"I am within God and God is within me. We are one unified whole. The sum total of all my thoughts, actions and beliefs is the way that God expresses itself through the unique gateway that is me, as a human channel."

EPILOGUE

THE SIMPLE TRUTHS

The pathway we are all upon is fundamentally called, "the great awakening". We are waking up from a deep slumber of forgetfulness.

In this most exciting arousal, we are remembering more of who we are and how to transition into this illumined state.

We can compare ourselves to the symbolic phoenix that rises out of its own ashes, reborn and renewed. We, too, are rising out of the confusing shadows and into the magnificence of our greater light.

As we advance into this divine expression, the human self remains grounded and intact. The difference is, that we now get to play in in a whole new way.

This new mode is more inclusive and more expansive. We can operate within a multitude of frequencies and dimensions of vibration. This shift is a complete game changer that brings ultimate liberation from the chains that bind.

The transition we are making is into our greater potential as an empowered Divine-Human. In other words, we are learning how to thrive as a divinely inspired human expression. This is a rich inner experience, which reflects as holistic integrity and wholeness.

This ultimately leads us into a practical emergence of the embodied state of divine immanence. To be operating from a state of divine immanence is to know, without any fiber of doubt, that the omnipresent nature of God permeates all aspects of your life.

When we do this for ourselves, we actually assist everyone else to do this as well. Our accomplishment of self-realization is very contagious and serves as a powerfully radiating force of love.

In these highly accelerating times, the path to self-realization no longer needs to be long and arduous. We no longer need to sit in caves or on mountaintops and meditate day and night. The shift we are making is into a new paradigm of thought.

This is a matrix shift, a new timeline that can easily be entered just as quickly as a shift in perception and a wink of the eye. Hopefully, this book has conveyed this idea clearly.

If there is anything out of this content that is the most important understanding of all, it is this truth.

You live, move and breathe inside the body of God, of absolute source. You have never ever been separated. You already are self-realized, liberated and free.

All is in a state of perfection, always. It is easy to think that it is not because the human consciousness perceives from beneath a veil of illusion.

It is purposed to be like this in the Earth schoolroom so that lessons can be learned and the soul can evolve.

Each and every person on this sacred planet is living out his or her evolutionary plan. Whether you achieve greatness or are stricken into the depths of despair, your life is on track.

There is great meaning behind every single thing that occurs. Whether you are a so-called saint or a sinner, you are learning exactly what you need to learn in this moment in time.

The program of duality is a powerful teacher.

The control of the ego is a powerful teacher.

The erratic emotions are a powerful teacher.

These guides serve us well in the material world. Sooner or later, however, we get the big knock on the door. When we hear that knock, we know the time has come to make the leap out of the jailhouse of distortion.

There is not one person who lives under the illusory veil that really knows with absolute certainty the full truth of God's plan. We can only trust in our higher power and follow its revealing messages as best we can.

Therefore, give great honor and highest respect to each other in this rather exotic walk in the Earthly sojourn.

THE SIMPLE
TRUTHS

The entire content of this book can be summarized into some very simple truths. To consistently live by these principles can elevate your life experiences into the supreme beatitude of being.

YOU ARE AN ASPECT OF GOD
IN THE FLESH

Your consciousness is born from and permanently resides within the vast macrocosmic body called God awareness, or existence itself; the primary source from which everything emanates.

This great Divine Presence that lives inside of you, is the same force of energy that creates everything from atoms and stars to the DNA of all life.

You are a microcosm made in the image of the macrocosm, an aspect of God outpictured in physical form.

Every man, woman and child is made in the image and likeness of the one original Creator of everything, at the most macro level.

All forms of life are birthed from this one primary source.

All is a reflection and a stepped down version of its greater aspect.

YOU ARE ALREADY SELF REALIZED, LIBERATED AND FREE

Divine Presence is your true nature. You are an imperishable, eternal and individualized identity that is also a part of every other human being.

As the highest aspect of your vast multidimensional constitution, the Divine Presence is the original seed of love and the immortal nucleus of your entire existence.

It is the originating source of every constructive impulse, thought, feeling, breath and action.

Its unifying, cohesive nature is the source of all of the love, wisdom and power required to overcome absolutely anything and everything that is of discordance and limitation.

The most beautiful realization of all is that your Divine Presence, as the greater you, is constantly extending its hand and providing you with an exact template to match.

This influencing reflection is what motivates your strongest passions and creative inspirations. It is what has brought you to be right here and right now.

You and this transcendent expression are one fused consciousness. There is no separation. You have always been self-realized. You already are divinely human.

DIVINE PRESENCE IS
YOUR GREATER SELF

Your Divine Presence is the non-physical component of yourself that acts as a conduit to all other dimensional aspects of yourself.

It is the intermediary that distills information from the spiritual realms in a way that you, the personality, can understand.

Once the mind and emotions are stable, this benevolent influence can work in collaboration with the personality.

It can help reorient the physical brain and entire consciousness to function through high states of coherence.

Through the higher mind, your Divine Presence can enable you to make decisions with utmost clarity and to know the truth, apart from any rationalization.

This inner guidance can speak and write through you without the use of the methodical brain, as you have been accustomed.

When you can authentically make contact with and cohere to the channel of the vaster self, expanded truths are revealed.

You become a 'knower'.

CONSCIOUSNESS IS NOT LOCATED IN THE BRAIN

Everything that occurs in your life is a reflection and a stepped down version of a greater flow of energy. Essentially, there is only one consciousness at play.

To evolve the perception, the one belief that must disintegrate concerns the idea that the consciousness is only located inside the physical world, perhaps somewhere in a person's brain.

You are much, much bigger than this!

Your consciousness actually exists outside of the physical body, even outside of this Earthly dimension.

Your consciousness is like a wave in the infinite ocean of universal awareness.

You are the entire universe and one small fragment of your consciousness is experiencing itself in the form of a human being.

Your unique consciousness existed before your human aspect was born; it has always existed and always will exist.

YOU ARE TRANSCENDING
THE PROGRAM OF DUALITY

The source of all is the Absolute, the universality of all manifestation.

This means that all pairs of opposites have the same foundation. Abundance and lack are from the same source as are light and dark, good and evil.

While different in frequency, they live on the same polarity spectrum and are extreme manifestations of the exact same energy.

The duality program is a gross perversion of the one and true unified reality.

The universe just is. It exists. It expresses as one unified and interconnected whole, bound through the principles of love, will and intelligence.

Creator, as Divine Presence in the physical reality, exists everywhere. It exists in the good things and also what is perceived as being bad.

It is up and down. It is on the right and the left. It is both light and the dark.

TRUTH IS FOUND IN
THE BIGGER PICTURE

Your Divine Presence is always communicating with you and supporting you, whether you realize it or not.

Everything in your life is perfectly unfolding according to your highest good on the path of soul evolution. There is no way you can make a mistake.

Rather than focusing on what you think you need to clear or heal, consider a different perspective. Maintain your focus only upon what you are doing, the bigger picture of your life.

In the absolute truth, all on the material place is one monumental outplay of divine orchestration.

Ultimately, it is all about you and the experiences that help your soul to learn its needed lessons to evolve.

Keep yourself attuned at all times to this bigger picture and dedicate all activity to your inspired thoughts and highest preferred outcome.

As a result, you just might experience a manifested reality precisely as you imagined.

You might also experience a much smoother process with it being effortlessly outlaid for you by an all-embracing higher power.

YOU ARE A GOD
ON TRAINING WHEELS

One of the best ways to rise out of limitation is to always remember that you are the creator in the physical reality.

Your current reality is a mirror to what is going on inside of you. It has manifested as a result of your innermost dominant thoughts.

Practice shifting your mind's default by consistently placing your focus upon the greater, with the highest version of who you really are.

Then, allow that greater self, your Divine Presence, to be the one and only navigator of your life.

Reality reflects your state of mind. State of mind reflects your reality.

PRESENCE IS THE
ALCHEMICAL STATE

You exist now, only in this now moment. This moment is your only home, past, present and future combined.

The embodied expression of Divine Presence requires the consciousness to be coherently connected in the space of 'now'. The present moment is where all creation occurs.

When you start leaning back and forth from now into future time or from now into past time, you are removing yourself from the purity of the eternal moment.

Then, all that you want to create and manifest for yourself cannot happen because you are not at home.

Free yourself from the mind that wants to define reality through the past or the future.

Things start to get really aligned when you hold clear definitions of who you are in the present moment.

'Now' is where you exist.

'Now' is the real.

INSPIRATION IS ALWAYS YOUR CUE

You can master the game of life simply by acting only upon whatever it is that you prefer and what gives you jubilant inspiration.

Inspiration comes from your Divine Presence. The manifesting doors will open so fast in response to you simply following your inspired feelings without hesitation.

When you act upon this inner feeling state, you actually ground and center in the now moment, a highly alchemical field from where all creation springs forth.

This instantly opens the door for more information to be revealed.

If you are not feeling inspired or are unsure how to proceed, clearly define what your highest preferences are in life, down to the simplest of things.

Then, prime the pump by just starting to live your preferred resonance.

A new day will dawn. Stress releases. Internal pressure goes away. The light naturally comes in because you are living your personal truth.

INTENTION PLUS ACTION BRINGS YOUR DREAMS TO LIFE

Action, along with positive intention, is what brings your dreams and innermost visions to life.

Only by taking actions that correspond with the clarity of intention will the universe know what to bring into your life.

When you take affirmative action steps, from the simplest to the grandest, you are sending a tremendous message to the universal creation field.

You set into motion the corresponding effects that mold your immediate future.

By affirming your intentions through positive daily action, a magnetic field of resonance completely shifts towards that intention. Impressive results will most likely be experienced.

This universal principle teaches you to be productive and an active co-creator in the manifestation process.

AS YOU PERCEIVE, LIFE EXPRESSES

Perception creates reality. Your world manifests according to how you choose to interpret it!

You can choose to live in a world that is perceived as full of division, hate, and separation. Alternatively, you can choose to live in a world that is perceived as loving, peaceful, and abundant.

Remember, you are made of divine essence. You are one with divine mind. You live inside the very body of absolute source. You are divinity through the form.

Command that you see only truth and only the truth can manifest. Keep your attention only upon what you want to manifest.

When you recognize perfection, you are that perfection. There is no other recognition.

It is all God. You, as an extension of that divinity, are the creator of your reality.

Once you understand these principles and master the thinking, your new creations take on majestic form because you know how reality works in a dense matter existence.

REFLECTIONS ARE YOUR
GREATEST BAROMETER

Life is created from your beliefs and the physical you is the sum total of all of your thoughts and feelings. Everything in your life is reflecting your thought vibration.

Whatever you are thinking, feeling and projecting, whether consciously or unconsciously, goes right into the mirror of physical reality.

This mirror responds by giving you back a reflection. These reflections form your life experiences.

You are in control of life's mirror by what you perceive to be true or what you believe you deserve.

As a powerful creator, to change any pictures in your manifesting reality, simply shift the thought that holds the belief in place.

You have to first make this change on the inside so that mirror of outer experience can reflect a different picture.

Learn to be the observer, in coherence with your life's reflections.

Through these reflections, you can make adjustments in your consciousness along the way.

HIGHER VIBRATIONS ALWAYS CONSUME THE LOWER

Higher frequencies always overcome the denser vibrations. Greater is more powerful than the lesser. The whole is more cohesive than the part.

By remaining in this divine attunement, you can walk in this world and not be swayed by conflict and divisive tendency. You can have a positive influence upon someone just through your energy presence alone.

As an extension of the unified reality, you can best assist those who are challenged by what you have *already* overcome. You now have the solution encoded in your energy field.

If you are in a role of assisting others to learn and evolve, it is often that the people who are attracted to you are the ones who will benefit by what you have already learned, healed and accomplished.

As you advance into greater vibrations of consciousness, you become a transforming presence everywhere you go.

In every handshake, in every hug, in every word, thought, feeling, and in every action, you are constantly transferring your imprinting out into the world.

You *are* Divine Presence.

EQUANIMITY IS AN
ENLIGHTENED STATE

The nature of life on the material plane is just a series of temporal reflections, always changing.

From this understanding, you can steadily make transition to living your life from the absolute reality. This is the unchanging, pure awareness of the vaster self.

In the absolute reality, there is only one consciousness. It exists in everything.

To make contact with and directly experience this one supreme consciousness in all things helps you to walk in the stilled poise of equanimity.

It is born from neutralized awareness.

When you are in neutralized awareness, you do not attach to the world; rather, you see the world for what it is, as a schoolroom for the soul.

There is no longer a charging impulse to give a quick opinion. The emoting self transitions into one of simply an observer as the duality of sides falls away.

You can be in the world but not be swallowed up by its human characters and conflicted realities.

STABILITY IS THE
TRANSFORMATIONAL IMPERATIVE

It is only at a certain stage in your development that the outward expression of the Divine Presence becomes active.

This is when the physical body, the emotional body and the egoic body are sufficiently balanced and stable to synthesize as one.

A more integrated personality is the result and one that becomes fully responsive to the inflowing energy of the Divine Presence.

This increased receptivity to the 'greater' happens when you think in wider and more inclusive terms.

Your Divine Presence experiences reality in an entirely different manner than the ego driven personality. It is fully aware of all other dimensions, timelines, potentials and probabilities.

Your ego self does not have this awareness.

To fully embody your expressive potential, it is imperative that you allow the dissolution of the ego's hold to happen.

This means to stabilize the monkey mind and its control over the free will.

THE GAME OF PLAYING
SMALL IS ENDING

In your transcendence from the dual plane, the ego is being retrained to serve as a follower and not the leader.

You are allowing the ego to relax and step aside so that another, more advanced intelligence can take the reins.

This takes focused surrender with constant reorientation to the heart and your childlike innocence. This foregoes the need to interpret things from the logic behind outplay.

When the mind stays in the purity of the heart, the names, the forms, the stories and even the personality begin to disappear.

The attaching bondage to the "I" or "me" gradually releases and the greater self emerges.

When attachment to the self-identity dissolves, so do the ideas that you must constantly clear and clear yourself, heal yourself or activate your self.

You release sabotaging patterns relating to the ways that the ego keeps you playing small.

YOU ARE ALWAYS TAKEN CARE OF AND SUPPORTED

Your Divine Presence is the God power. It governs all manifestation in your life perfectly. It is the power producing it and the force sustaining it.

When you stand unified with this divine principle, all is magnetized to you in spontaneous flow, in perfect timing, and in just the right quantity.

No strenuous effort is required. No affirmations are needed. Even the idea of prayer becomes obsolete. "Want" and "need" become signals to what is already in manifesting motion.

Everything is always here and always present. The moment you recognize a need, it is already being fulfilled. It is absolutely impossible to need anything if it were not already in existence.

This is indicated by the very fact that "need" has shown up and is expressing. You confidently accept the fact implied in the need that the solution is already coming towards you.

If it were not already in momentum, the thought would not even enter into your awareness.

You do not have to go out there so aggressively and get it. You do not have to force something to happen.

IT IS THROUGH THE ACT OF GIVING THAT YOU SHALL RECEIVE

The Law of Generosity is one of the main governing principles to realize an emergence of global unity and peace upon the Earth.

As you express divine love in service to others, you help release creation's unlimited storehouse of supply.

If you truly love, you cannot help but give. To give is to expand and thus the Law of Love is fulfilled.

With no expectation of return as a result of giving, it is impossible to avoid receiving. The energy is returned to you, amplified, through the natural fulfillment of the law.

As you come to live in greater alignment with this governing principle, all sense of lack eventually evaporates.

This is because you humbly know that it is through the act of giving that you shall receive.

SELF-LOVE IS THE GATEWAY
TO DIVINE INTIMACY

To be in divine intimacy is one of the highest attainable states possible for the human experience.

Your presence and your very existence is founded upon the surrender to your one and true Beloved.

This is speaking into a union of love with your Creator. The nature of this force of love is to expand, and to such a degree that it naturally spills over to have an immense influence on those around you.

To arrive into this level of deep intimacy with the God within, one must first have intimacy with the self. This refers to truly loving the self, fully and completely.

Self-validation, self-respect and self-acknowledgement puts you right in touch with the Divine Presence of your being.

To love yourself at the deepest level is to simultaneously know and experience the Divine Presence manifesting in your life.

As a result, this becomes the pure mirror of your thought energy.

INTEGRITY IS YOUR
SUSTAINABLE POWER

In phases of divine embodiment, increasing levels of integrity provide the springboard into your greater self.

This means that your entire energy field, including the physical, emotional, mental and spiritual bodies, is unified and working synergistically.

Your thoughts match your feelings; your feelings match your actions. You 'walk your talk' in every way.

Through the quality of integrity, you create life reflections that mirror this holistic blending. This is true power!

In whatever way you view yourself; you will likewise see the world. If you are separated and disconnected within, this will be your perception of external reality.

If you are one with your totality, perceiving yourself and your creator as unified and working together, your life will function holistically and with a high degree of sustainability.

You will experience a reality that is peaceful and purposeful and one that expresses abundance on every level of your life.

This is the true meaning of divine embodiment. You operate from integrity, whole and undivided with yourself and with your supreme source.

YOU ARE SUPREMELY BLESSED

The love of your Divine Presence is all-giving and is always showering its gifts upon you.

Remember this one truth and you will naturally be without self-serving desires.

You will know that all of your needs are taken care of at all times.

There will be no addictions or compulsions. Greed will vanish. The seeking goes away. The heart opens even wider. The spirit of generosity emerges.

Active service in the spirit of generosity is one of the most significant understandings to realizing the self as part of the benevolent God force.

This is when you come to realize true selflessness. Every activity, including your thoughts, feelings, words and acts, becomes centered upon service and giving.

In this turning point of your evolution, you are motivated by love and love alone to carry out a much greater Will upon the Earth.

THE PERFECTION OF DIVINE PRESENCE IS OMNIPRESENT

One of the greatest services that you can give to evolving humanity is to see the perfection of the Divine Presence in everything.

When the thought of the Divine is held while carrying out your daily life activities, this supreme energy percolates into your personality. It starts expressing in your actions, feelings, and speech.

This is the manifestation of the common expression, "bringing Heaven to Earth." The Divine is entering from the most expanded planes of consciousness to express through you in daily life.

This evolved perception, where there is no judgment or separation, *is* the ascending consciousness.

You are undergoing a dimensional consciousness shift that takes you into a completely new way of living and perceiving.

It is as simple as this; you are seeing, feeling and being as the Divine Presence in your daily life, *always.*

Your synthesis with this greater momentum gives you incredible ability to magnetize and accomplish as one with the pure, illuminating spirit of all life.

"When I am at one and in coherence with my Divine Presence, I am led down the path of non-stop opening doors. To be attuned to my greater self is to know that I am an aspect of Absolute Source, the supreme entity experiencing Itself through my physical form."

GLOSSARY

Absolute Consciousness

The entire universe is propelled through the energy of a infinitely expanding field of intelligence of which everything and everyone is an integral part. This refers to the interpenetration of a supreme, all-pervading, intelligent and loving force of source energy within and throughout all manifested creation. It is referred to by many names including God, Prime Creator, Brahma, Allah, Great Spirit.

Antahkarana

This is a Sanskrit word that means the totality of two levels of mind. It can be viewed as an energetic bridge that connects the personality mind with the vastness of one's multidimensional awareness. The building of this bridge helps us to be consciously responsive to impressions from the many dimensions of Divine Presence.

Attunement

To be in attunement is to feel in harmony with, and at one, with another being or subject matter. Whole self-attunement means to have strong connection with our all-inclusive holistic nature.

Code, Human

Our body functions through detailed encoding. This code expresses as the ordering of nucleotides in the DNA molecules, which carries the informative data for cellular activity. The genes inside the cell's nucleus are strung together in such a way that their coded sequence conveys our entire human expression, including what we inherit from our parents and ancestors.

Coherence

Coherence is the foundational base to our evolutionary advancement as a human species. To be coherently connected is to be aligned with the greater whole that is influencing our lives and entire existence. Holistic coherence evokes harmony, interconnectivity and stabilized order, where the whole is greater and more efficient than the sum of its parts.

Crystalline Grid

This is a term used to describe the complex grid-like pathway or matrix of high-frequency energy that is part of the Earth's energetic architecture. Likened to a spiritual telecommunications system, its pathways of light help us connect, etherically and telepathically, to the higher consciousness of humans all over the world.

Dark Night of the Soul

This a highly transformational phase of soul initiation that is initially accompanied with a period of intense suffering while so much of the held illusion, such as emotional glamour, personal desires, fantasies and false ideals, is illuminated. It can involve the breakdown of the ego, negativity and many other distortions. The spiritual initiate, enmeshed in these traps, is required to free the self from the mental and emotional bondage.

Divine - Divinity

This pertains to, or proceeds from, a state of perfection, supreme beauty and absolute wholeness. This is magnificence and excellence in the highest degree. Divinity is the state of being Divine, the core essence and inherent nature of every single soul incarnated upon the Earth.

Divine Channel

Benevolent spiritual influences from the higher realms use people and their energetic body as conduits through which to transfer influential energy to positively assist others. Divine Channels serve from the qualities of highest integrity, self-validation and a centered presence.

Divine Embodiment

To embody the divine means to personify, exemplify and give tangible form to your greatest spiritual presence. You are merging back, consciously, with the source of your existence.

Divine Immanence

This refers to the human's innate divine nature as a magnificent being of pure awareness. The Divine Presence is within each and every person as part of their totality of consciousness. To be operating from a state of divine immanence is to know, without any fiber of doubt, that the omnipresent and all-powerful nature of God permeates all aspects of your life.

Divine Intimacy

This is speaking into a union of love with your Creator. The nature of this force of love is to expand, and to such a degree that it naturally spills over to have an immense influence on those around you. To be in divine intimacy is one of the highest attainable states possible for the human experience.

Divine Love

The very nature of divine love surpasses all human description. This book conveys it as wielding the cohesive power that guides the universe, leading and sustaining everything into integration, unity and inclusiveness. This radiant field of intelligence knows no opposite nor does it come from a place of need. It is a neutralizing, cohesive force and its transforming power is boundless. At the human level, it is love for the whole of life.

Divine Presence (Greater Self)

God, expressing as the Divine Presence within you, is the authority of the entire universe. As the highest aspect of your vast multidimensional constitution, the Divine Presence is the original seed of love and the immortal nucleus of your entire existence. It is the originating source of every constructive impulse, thought, feeling, breath and action. The Divine Presence is your greater self and who you are as a totality of consciousness.

Divine Principles (Universal Laws)

They are the governing forces that determine every aspect of creation and by which everything in the Universe is governed. These are the laws of nature that are the foundation stones upon which humanity's new framework of consciousness is built Knowing these universal laws, or divine principles, is fundamental to changing the circumstances of your life so that you can consciously create your intended reality and achieve true self-mastery.

Divine Will

Divine Will is the driving consciousness behind all creation and is responsible for the natural unfolding of the evolutionary plan. This living forcefield penetrates through to the core of all things, guiding the evolution of human intelligence. Calling it into your life creates an enormous infusion of spiritual energy that awakens and illuminates the consciousness.

DNA

Deoxyribonucleic acid, or DNA, is a molecule that contains the instructions for an organism to develop and function. The human DNA code is rearranged in billions of different sequences to form our unique blueprint for life.

Duality

Duality is a false program of perception created through the human ego and continually fed by its fears. It is the duality within us that is in resistance to another aspect of itself, due to a mind-set that perceives from separation. Duality divides; it's either one thing or the other. From duality perception, we formulate self-attaching desires and opinions; all from the separated self.

Ego, Human

The human ego can be defined as that self-conscious aspect of the human personality that is identified as the "I". Your ego makes contact with the external world through perception. It is that part of you that perceives itself as being separated from everything else. It constantly competes with your spirit for control over the inner voice.

Emotional Glamour

Glamour is emotion driven desire colorizing itself on an illusory screen through the lens of the conditioned human personality. These illusory forms enliven our lives, sometimes with ecstatic sensations, however, they produce limiting consciousness patterns. This can outplay in fantasized realities, false values, misleading desires, distorted perceptions and many needless necessities.

Equanimity

Equanimity is the state of inner stability arising from a deep awareness and the acceptance of what each moment is presenting. From this composure, we live life in the eternal now with an evenness of mind that is undisturbed and unattached to anything of the temporary world.

God

The entire universe is propelled through the energy of a infinitely expanding field of intelligence of which everything and everyone is an integral part. This refers to the interpenetration of a supreme, all-pervading, intelligent and loving force of source energy within and throughout all manifested creation. It is referred to by many names including Absolute Source, Prime Creator, Brahma, Allah, Great Spirit.

Grace

Grace is the infused presence and power of God made manifest in the human realm. It is felt as a divine blessing and it comes to us in many ways and from all dimensions. Grace is the effect of divine love in action and it permeates all existence.

Greater Self (Divine Presence)

The Divine Presence is your greater self that facilitates the awakening of your human consciousness. God, expressing as the Divine Presence within you, is the authority of the entire universe. As the highest aspect of your vast multidimensional constitution, the Divine Presence is the original seed of love and the immortal nucleus of your entire existence. This is the nonphysical component of your human embodiment that serves as a conduit to all other versions and dimensions of your one total and very vast self.

Higher Mind (Higher Mental Body)

The term is used to mean that part of the mental faculty that connects and links the human soul to the dimension of unified awareness. The higher mental body is a part of your auric field together with other energetic layers such as the emotional body and etheric body. It is the vehicle of expression for the thinking human intelligence. It influences the thoughts, perceptions and mental processes.

Initiation, Path of Spiritual

This highly customized plan for each person's advancement occurs through successive stages of consciousness awakening, which support remembrance and re-unification. This puts a person face to face with the many temptations of life. This can be like a series of tests to determine how the gift of personal free will is adeptly handled. It was designed by the guardians of the race to guarantee the surest and most accelerated method for human evolution from the Earth plane and its dense facade of separation.

Initiation, Spiritual

Initiation is an organic, gradual expansion of consciousness, a process of soul evolution in which successive stages of unification take place. This involves the relinquishing of all separate reactions in a series of progressive renunciations to achieve reunification with Source. Initiation is the planetary right of all sentient beings.

Inspiration (Divine)

The divine guidance that is exerted directly upon the mind and soul of humankind. To be divinely inspired means that the human mind has reached a stage where it is consciously and positively under the direction of its higher aspect of self.

Integrity

This is the state of being whole and undivided. It is the quality of being honest and having strong moral principles. Other descriptive words are sincere, virtuous, honorable, truthful and trustworthiness. To be divinely embodied, you are holistically integrated from within.

Intuition, Spiritual

This level of intuition is direct knowing. It is tapping into the realms of truth at the level of source consciousness. To be intuitive is to have an open pathway through which the higher mind transfers pure knowledge.

Law of Action

This principle states that when appropriate action is exerted upon our intentions and desires, an inevitable reaction is experienced.

COMING HOME TO DIVINE PRESENCE

To take action means to take the actual physical steps towards the desired outcome. Action, along with positive intention, is what brings our dreams and innermost visions to life.

Law of Generosity

This is also the Law of Cause and Effect, which conveys, "as you sow, so shall you reap", or, "what comes around goes around". Every action we put out generates a force of energy that returns to us in like kind. The purity of our greater love gives constantly as its inherent nature, requiring nothing back in return. With no expectation of return as a result of giving, it is impossible to avoid receiving. The energy is returned to us, amplified, through the natural fulfillment of the law.

Law of Love

This principle conveys that God is love and we are expressions of that love. As we express this love in service to the whole of life, we release creation's unlimited storehouse of supply. If we truly love, we cannot help but give. To give is to expand and thus the Law of Love is fulfilled.

Morphogenetic Fields

This term is used to identify the developmental blueprints for species types. Simply put, they program our future. All conscious creation, from micro to macro, is manifested through these imprinting field templates. They are influenced by the collective consciousness of that level of species.

Multidimensional Intelligence

This is the state of awareness that perceives beyond the physical form and what the human senses are reading to the brain. Cognition comes from expanded sense perception. There is attunement with many aspects of existence and from many dimensions of awareness.

Mystery Schools

Until this current age, mystery schools protected and guarded the keys to enlightenment. There was a time when spiritual subject matter was considered taboo. There was a great need to protect the ancient knowledge from the sinister forces that attempted to eliminate these sacred teachings from the Earth.

Omnipresence

This is the ability to be present in all places at all times and through the consciousness alone. Familiarity with the term omnipresence comes from its reference as an attribute of a supreme being. It is commonly linked with omnipotence, omniscience and being eternal.

Perception

Perception is generally described in the dictionaries as the interpretation of sensory information in order to represent and understand one's life and the environment. Multidimensional perception is to have the ability to perceive beyond the five human senses.

Pineal Gland

The pineal gland is an important endocrine gland in the brain. Its purpose, as a light receptor, is to translate incoming frequencies of light and then send out encoded messages through the hormonal pathways. Known as the third eye, the pineal gland is a perceptual doorway through which greater dimensions of awareness can be experienced.

Polarity

Polarity is the difference between the two extremes of one thing. The law of polarity says that everything can be separated into two wholly opposite parts; yet, each of these parts still contains the potentiality of the other. It is all in how it is perceived.

COMING HOME TO DIVINE PRESENCE

Principle of Correspondence

This principle speaks to the mirror-image relationship between all that exists in creation. It conveys that, in all existence, the common interweaving threads between the dimensions of manifestation are harmony, agreement and correspondence. Everything is a microcosm of the macrocosm. We see the same patterns reproduced in all levels of the cosmos, from the largest scale all the way down to the smallest sub-atomic substance, including the metaphysical.

Self-Actualization

This is the actual realization or fulfillment of one's highest potential, talents and/or abilities. In this book, the term means to realize the greater self-expression.

Self-Realization

This is a term derived from eastern and yoga philosophies and many spiritual schools of thought. This is a state in which an individual knows who they truly are and their oneness with Source, as Source. They have reached their highest potential in the human embodiment, moving beyond fears and self-delusion and into the mastery over the matter world.

Self-Validation

Self-validation is accepting yourself, your thoughts and feelings as real and true for you. This means to consistently validate all of your experiences and situations as a blessing, full of meaning and an orchestration for your highest good. Invalidation results from the consciousness programming that tenaciously holds on to the negative perceptions about the personal self.

Soul

The soul is the linking or middle principle, representing the relation between spirit and matter. It is the link between God and the human form. The soul provides consciousness, character and quality to all manifestations in form. It also serves as the inner guide of the human personality.

Soul Fusion

This is the phase of spiritual awakening when the human personality and the incarnated soul fuse to become one unified entity. It is then that a refined and more 'soulful' personality assumes the dominant position in life and is charged with a great sense of purpose.

Spiritual Aspirant

This is someone who aspires to advance his or her consciousness in the area of spiritual development. This puts the individual on the path of spiritual initiation.

Starseed (Archetype)

It is through the Starseed archetype that we acknowledge our origins from the stars and connection to all that is. Starseed symbolically represents a soul that incarnates specifically to assist in humanity's evolution. They usually come with immense amount of knowledge, talent and ability, however, these attributes can be veiled. Starseeds often endure a challenging path of life initiation due to their primary missive to serve as a leader and wayshower while helping to create new pathways for others to follow. As the name implies, starseeds are "seeded" and carry the evolutionary ascension codes. They have garnered experiences elsewhere in the universe including the Earth schoolroom.

Transfiguration, Personality

In general, transfiguration means to change in form or appearance. In this text, transfiguration is a multi-layered process of purification through which our human personality fuses with the light of the soul. This marks a time of great transformation and the stage in our spiritual development when the outward expression of the Divine Presence becomes active.

Universal Laws (Divine Principles)

They are the governing forces that determine every aspect of creation and by which everything in the universe is governed. These are the laws of nature that are the foundation stones upon which humanity's new framework of consciousness is built. Knowing these universal laws, or divine principles, is fundamental to changing the circumstances of your life so that you can consciously create your intended reality and achieve true self-mastery.

Vibration

In its simplest form, vibration is the rate of oscillation around an equilibrium position. At a spiritual level, vibration is the rate of spin of the electrons as they move around the nucleus of the atom. This rate increases when there is more coherent light within the cells.

ABOUT THE AUTHOR

Tiara Kumara is a multifaceted educator whose global work and educational offerings has profoundly assisted numerous lives in spiritual advancement and consciousness empowerment.

As a dedicated spiritual teacher, Tiara is the founding producer of I AM Avatar (*IAMAvatar.org*), Guided Audio Meditations (*GuidedAudioMeditations.com*), and several educational courses that support phases of self-realization.

Her transforming programs are known to give great acceleration for individuals to authentically embody their greater potential and the highly influential abilities that are born from this resonance.

Empowered by the teachings of some of the greatest spiritual masters, Tiara has endured impressive training for her teaching role and one that brings a high degree of integrity and stamina to the work.

She is an avid global traveler and has been greatly influenced by metaphysical studies, esoteric experiences, shamanic practices and the principles of unification.

Tiara has an extensive background in alternative health therapies and the healing arts.

Websites:

IAMAvatar.org
GuidedAudioMeditations.com

Made in United States
North Haven, CT
25 September 2024

57895013R00153